# The New York Times
# Cooking

# No-Recipe Recipes

## Sam Sifton

Photographs by David Malosh
and Food Styling by Simon Andrews

TEN SPEED PRESS
California | New York

# Contents

# Recipes

## The Staples Sisters: Rice and Pasta

# You Don't Need a Recipe

As an editor at The New York Times and in particular as the founding editor of NYT Cooking, our digital cookbook and cooking site, I spend a lot of time bringing together cooks, reporters, chefs, and critics to lay out strict instructions for how best to prepare specific dishes. These recipes take a particular form: a list of ingredients and measurements that are followed by step-by-step directions for how to use them to result in a finished dish. I think of these recipes as sheet music, a form of notation that allows home cooks to re-create the cooking of others, just as a printed chord chart allows Mike from Sheboygan to play the Beatles' repertoire in his den, passingly well.

But I don't just cook with recipes, and I am not alone. Indeed, cooking without recipes is a kitchen skill, same as cutting vegetables into dice or flipping an omelet. It's a proficiency to develop, a way to improve your confidence in the kitchen and makes the act of cooking fun when it sometimes seems like a chore.

Since 2015, I have included one of these no-recipe recipes—an invitation for you to improvise in the kitchen—in every Wednesday edition of "What to Cook," the newsletter I write for The Times. What follows are some highlights from that archive, suggestions for things you might cook for yourself or for as many people you have or don't have at the table, anytime.

# You Do Need a Pantry

Here's how I used to cook, before no-recipe recipes: I'd shop for every meal. I'd leave the office in the evening and stroll to the market to pick up the ingredients necessary to make whatever recipe I had chosen to make, and I'd use those ingredients to cook my meal.

This felt very Parisian, but really all I was doing was assembling meal kits. If I needed sesame oil, I'd buy a small bottle. If I needed garlic, I'd buy a small head. I'd buy two large potatoes for four people, and a little onion to go with them. My cabinets had some staples in them, but not many. I did not always have a tub of gochujang in the refrigerator, a jar of chili crisp, a container of oil-cured olives. I sometimes was without anchovies, without tahini, without roasted peanuts, without Parmesan. Often there were no eggs.

That is no longer the case, and it should not be the case for you, if you'd like to join me in cooking this new, improvisational way, without recipes. You do not need a recipe. But you must have staple supplies on hand with which to cook. What follows is a list of my most common kitchen companions. It's just a start. You will add to the list as your tastes and interests dictate.

**Alliums.** Your cooking will benefit from always having onions and garlic, scallions most of the time, shallots sometimes, leeks occasionally, and chives once in a while.

**Baking staples.** No-recipe baking recipes fail fairly reliably; there's science to baking, after all. But flour and cornstarch are important to have on hand for building savory sauces and dusting things you're going to fry.

**Beans.** There's no question that dried beans make for delicious bean pots, but for the purposes of no-recipe recipe making, I always have a few cans of black beans, white beans, red kidney beans, and some garbanzos as well. Any of these can be transformed into an excellent dinner, no recipe required.

**Butter.** I use a lot of butter in my cooking and hope that you will, too. It keeps forever in the fridge and even longer in the freezer. I prefer unsalted for cooking and desserts and salted for toast.

**Canned fish.** Anchovies play an important role in a lot of no-recipe recipes, and you can always make tuna salad if you have a can. I keep canned clams on hand as well, for pasta and pizza experiments. And if you're really in a pinch, sardines are a pleasant meal, on crackers.

**Cheese.** You'll see Parmesan in a lot of the suggestions for meals in this book. I like keeping blocks of Cheddar in the refrigerator and some of low-moisture mozzarella. Provolone is good to have. So is blue cheese. And feta. But if all you have is Parmesan, you'll survive and happily, too.

**Cured meats.** Bacon is at the heart of a lot of my bean cooking, and diced salami in a tomato sauce is always a winner. You can use cured meats to flavor meatloaf, enhance salads, and build out sandwiches. Ham's a secret weapon. You should always have cured meats in the refrigerator.

**Dried fruit and nuts.** Salad savers. Rice enhancers. A handful of roasted peanuts on your fried rice will take you far.

**Eggs.** There are very few no-recipe recipes that are not improved by adding an egg: fried, soft-boiled, scrambled, poached.

**Oils.** Olive oil, including extra virgin for finishing a dish. A neutral oil with a high smoke point, like canola. Sesame oil. All will come in handy as you cook.

**Pasta.** I keep a number of boxes of different shapes and sizes of pasta on hand——spaghetti and shells in particular—and I always have a tray of cheese ravioli in the freezer, just in case, and an accompanying package of the dumplings some call pot stickers. Egg noodles are a fine thing to have around as well, and always a few packets of instant ramen against the need for an emergency meal.

**Rice.** I like having plain long-grain white rice in the cupboard, along with Arborio rice for risotto, jasmine and basmati rice for their aroma and flavor, brown rice for kids home from college, and wild rice for those nights when nuttiness is required.

**Stock.** Maybe you'll get to the point where you have ice-cube trays in the freezer filled with double-strength chicken stock, fish stock, veal stock. But in the meantime, laying in some bouillon paste or boxed stock is never in error.

**Sugars.** Brown sugar, honey, maple syrup, and molasses can punch up a spicy-salty sauce quite well.

**Vegetables.** It's good to have a carrot when you decide you need one. Likewise potatoes and celery. A few bags of frozen peas will come in handy, as will frozen corn. Canned tomatoes are a godsend. So, too, is tomato paste.

And, now, for herbs, spices, and condiments. Here's a list of what's always in my house, representative of the kind of cooking I do, and that I've laid out in this book. Your list may end up looking very different. It's just important that it's a generous list. Herbs, spices, and condiments are at the very heart of no-recipe cooking.

## Herbs and Spices

Bay leaves

Black pepper

Chile powder

Cinnamon sticks

Curry powder

Dried rosemary

Dried sage

Dried thyme

Furikake

Ground cumin

Kosher salt

Red pepper flakes

Smoked paprika

## Condiments

Capers

Chili crisp

Chutney

Fish sauce

Gochujang

Hoisin sauce

Hot sauce

Ketchup

Mayonnaise

Miso

Mustard

Olives

Oyster sauce

Pickles—any and all fermented vegetables apply

Rice wine

Sour cream

Soy sauce

Sriracha

Tahini

Vinegars—red, black, balsamic, rice

Worcestershire sauce

Yogurt

# Always, a Party Board

Cheese

Cured meats

Condiments

Crackers or bread

Vegetables

Olives

Olive oil

Vinegar

You don't need a recipe for a party board, ever. The chef Gabrielle Hamilton calls the assemblage a "snack tray." In the name of romance, she once stacked Pringles on one, with a ramekin of Castelvetrano olives. Her swain, now her wife, Ashley Merriman, responded by adding, according to Hamilton, "pepperoni cut as thin as fish scales and shingled just as neatly."

You need only what cheese is in the refrigerator, sliced or wedged or cubed, along with cured meats— I like rolled mortadella, spread inside with a little mayonnaise and dotted with pickled jalapeño—and a little bread or pile of crackers. Maybe add some cherry tomatoes, halved and tossed in olive oil and good vinegar, with salt and pepper? You could stuff them with mozzarella, if you have the time. Or celery, cut into batons? Carrots, likewise? Raw or roasted peppers, sliced? How about a small bowl of olives? You could go with Jarlsberg, Triscuits, and vodka sodas. Or smoked salmon, shaved asparagus, and some crème fraîche with chives, dill, and tarragon. A party board is whatever you want.

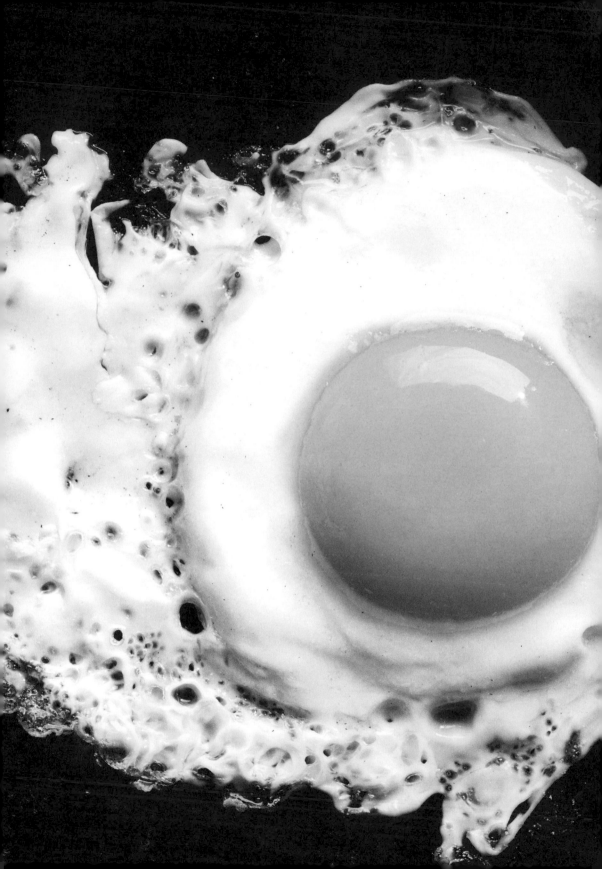

**Breakfast, Anytime**

# Peanut Butter Smoothie

One morning, one of my kids asked for this. I said, "What?" She told me what might be in it. I listened and then I jammed. Turns out it's like a morning frappé: slightly savory, really good.

Bananas

Peanut butter

Milk

Maple syrup

Take a couple of bananas, a big scoop of peanut butter, a couple big glugs of milk, a couple drops of maple syrup, and a whole bunch of ice. Blitz that in your blender or food processor and enjoy.

**Tip**

If you make this sort of thing a lot, it might be time for a blender upgrade, to what's called a high-performance blender. In the smoothie game, a high-performance blender is a crucial tool.

**Modifications**

Oat milk for the whole milk works just great. So does a handful of cashews for the peanut butter.

# Chilled Oranges with Yogurt

A breakfast of champions! Take a few navel oranges and put them in the fridge overnight. Slice them into eighths in the morning and eat them standing over the sink, before you've even made coffee or tea. Then tell me if there's a better-tasting fruit available, save a perfect watermelon or, like, three mangoes a year.

Navel oranges

Yogurt

Mint

Here's a way to make those oranges even better, so that you might even serve them for dessert: Peel them, segment them, cut the segments into pieces. Stir the pieces into full-fat plain yogurt that is maybe not Greek yogurt because Greek yogurt is a little thick. Add a few torn mint leaves and everyone will remember it for a very long time.

# Soft-Boiled Eggs with Anchovy Toast

If you're up for a delicious, slightly sporty breakfast tomorrow, you might consider making some anchovy butter tonight. Then, come morning, you can slather toast with the result and serve it with soft-boiled eggs, a breakfast I once had in London at a hotel and restaurant the chef Fergus Henderson was running in Leicester Square.

Butter

Anchovies

Garlic

Paprika

Lemon

Bread

Eggs

Chives

Take a stick of unsalted butter and let it soften on the counter while you assemble the other ingredients: a tin of rinsed and minced anchovies, some minced garlic cloves, a shake or two of smoked or regular paprika, a wee squirt of lemon juice, and, maybe but probably not, some salt. Fork everything together into the butter.

Toast your bread. Make sure you spread the butter "wall to wall" on the toast. That means to cover the entire surface of the bread from edge to edge—an important step in buttering, one that is too often shirked. Place however many eggs you want to cook in a small saucepan and cover with lukewarm water. Over high heat, bring the water just to a boil, then turn off the heat, cover the pan, and let stand for a minute or so. Transfer the egg pan to the sink and run cold water over the eggs for about 30 seconds, then peel them and place them on your toast. Sprinkle minced chives over and, well, you know what to do.

# Kaya Toast with Eggs

Kaya toast and eggs is a Singapore tradition: toasted light-brown bread covered with the coconut-milk custard jam known as kaya plus a pat of salted butter, served with soft-boiled eggs cracked into a bowl with soy sauce. Dip the sweet-salty-crisp-soft bread into the salt-and-peppery umami creaminess of the eggs.

Eggs

Bread

Kaya

Butter

Soy sauce

White pepper

Place however many eggs you want to cook in a small saucepan and cover with lukewarm water. Over high heat, bring the water just to a boil, then turn off the heat, cover the pan, and let stand for a minute or so. Toast your bread. Spread with kaya and top with butter. Sandwich the toasts, if you like. Transfer the egg pan to the sink and run cold water over the eggs for about 30 seconds, then peel them into your bowl. Add dark soy sauce, a healthy shake of white pepper, and stir together. Get to 'em with the toast.

**Tip**

When boiling eggs, you put them in lukewarm water to start because if you slide cold eggs into hot water, the shells will crack.

**Modification**

Honey or marmalade is a totally acceptable hack for the kaya.

# Savory French Toast with Cherry Tomatoes and Basil

It's axiomatic that a stash of leftover bread makes the best French toast for breakfast, and so it stands to reason that a savory version would be equally satisfying for the crew around your dinner table. At least that's true in my house.

Eggs

Basil

Hot sauce

Bread

Butter

Cherry tomatoes

Basil

Whisk the eggs in a shallow bowl as you usually would for French toast, but omit any sugar and cinnamon, and instead hit the eggs with pepper, chopped basil, and a dash of hot sauce. Slide some slices of old bread in there to soak, then fry up the toasts in butter. Scattering a few handfuls of halved cherry tomatoes into the pan as the bread cooks yields a fine topping. Sprinkle basil leaves over. Doubters will doubt no more.

# French Toast Hash

An exceptional breakfast feast.

Baguette

Eggs

Milk

Butter

Breakfast sausages

Apples

Maple syrup

Slice a baguette into inch-thick slices. Whisk together the eggs and a splash of milk in a shallow bowl, perhaps with a dash of vanilla and definitely a little bit of salt. Soak the bread in the egg mixture for a time, shaking the bowl a few times to encourage absorption. Then melt some butter in a big pan and fry the bread until golden brown on both sides. Transfer to a casserole dish and put it in a low oven to stay warm. Melt some more butter in the pan and cook some sausages. Put those in the oven with the toasts. Slice a few apples and fry them in the fat remaining in the pan. Scatter those on top of the toasts and sausages, drizzle the whole situation with a little maple syrup, and, if you're feeling fancy, dust with confectioners' sugar.

**Tip**

French toast is known in France as *pain perdu,* which translates to "lost bread." It is made with stale loaves that would otherwise get discarded. So use stale bread, if you have it. But I find my bread goes too quickly for that to happen, so most often I make this with bread that's not quite lost.

The New York Times Cooking No-Recipe Recipes

# Fried Egg Quesadilla

This simple fried-egg quesadilla makes as fine a light supper as it does a breakfast.

Butter

Corn tortillas

Cheddar

Cilantro

Hot sauce

Egg

Melt some butter in a pan and gently cook a tortilla in it. Top the tortilla with grated Cheddar, a little chopped cilantro, hot sauce, and another tortilla. Cook, flipping the quesadilla a few times, until it is crisp and golden and the cheese has melted into lace at the edges. Use a spatula to pull it out of the pan, and place it on a cutting board to rest. Fry an egg in the pan with a little more butter. Cut the quesadilla into quarters, transfer to a plate, and place the egg on top. Sprinkle with more cilantro and hot sauce.

**Modifications**

Top the Cheddar with a slice of deli ham or some cooked bacon, if you want them. Swap a spoonful of salsa for the hot sauce.

# Roasted Cauliflower Soup with Artichoke Cream

Here's a simple, rich, amazingly creamy soup, relatively quickly made.

Cauliflower

Olive oil

Garlic

Canned artichoke hearts

Stock or milk

Parmesan

Roast a whole head of cauliflower in a pot in a 400°F oven with a drizzle of olive oil, some salt and pepper, and a few cloves of garlic. When the cauliflower is all soft on the inside and crisp on the outside and good to go—45 minutes or so—cut it into pieces and whiz them up in a blender with a can of drained artichoke hearts and a little chicken stock, vegetable stock, or milk. Blend in some grated Parmesan at the end. Yowza.

**Tip**

Trim the greens from the stalk of the cauliflower, but don't cut out the stalk itself. It brings big flavor.

**Modifications**

Roast a couple of anchovies with the cauliflower, if you like their umami pop. Roast a carrot or two along with the cauliflower and use in place of the artichoke hearts. Use Cheddar in place of the Parmesan.

# Celery Soup

I first had a tricked-out version of this soup at the Lost Kitchen in Freedom, Maine, in a dining room warm and glowing with candlelight and decency. The celery was cooked in olive oil with alliums, and new potatoes for heft, and the whole thing got whizzed into a kind of pale-green perfection. I made a cover-band version at home. So can you.

Celery

Olive oil

Onion

Vegetable stock

Cut up a whole head of celery, reserving the leaves, and sauté the cut sections in a generous amount of olive oil with sliced onion. Don't put any color on them. Just get everything soft, then put it in a food processor with a little vegetable stock. When the mixture is smooth, return it to a pot on the stove and heat it through, with a little more stock, if necessary. Serve garnished with the celery leaves and a shower of pepper.

## Tip

My general advice when it comes to ingredients—use the best available at your price point and store—absolutely applies when it comes to celery. Try the organic. You'll see.

## Modifications

Swap in scallions, leeks, shallots, or a lot of chives for the onions. Use cream instead of stock. At the Lost Kitchen, the soup came with dabs of homemade ricotta and fresh-picked crab. You could serve it over a lump of meh ricotta and canned crab from the tinned fish section of the supermarket and still get great results.

# Split Pea Soup

Here's a 60-minute pressure-cooker homage to a soup that used to be served at Roberta's in Brooklyn. Serve with a hunk of baguette and some salted butter.

Onion

Carrot

Neutral oil

Split peas

Smoked pig's trotters

Bay leaf

Beer

Sauté chopped onion and carrot in oil in the bottom of a pressure-cooker pot, then add a pound of split peas, a couple of smoked trotters, a bay leaf, the better part of a tallboy or bottle of beer, and a little less than a quart of water. Close up and cook under pressure for 45 minutes. Releasing the steam manually amazingly transforms the peas into a thick puree, the Greek yogurt of soups. Then strip the meat from the trotters and put it back into the pot, season with salt and pepper, and heat through. (You may want to thin the soup a little with water or stock.) When you're done eating, you'll be bowing like Hugh Jackman at a curtain call. At least in your mind!

**Tip**

To make split pea soup, the general ratio is half a pound (a cup) split peas to about a quart of liquid.

**Modifications**

Use a ham hock instead of trotters. Or sub smoked turkey wings or a neck for the ham, if you like. Or, if you roast a duck sometime, make this soup with the carcass afterward. Oh, my. And you needn't cook with beer. Chicken stock works just as well.

# Speedy Fish Chowder

For this fast and elegant stew, you'll need something in the neighborhood of a quarter to half pound of fish fillets per person. Serve with crusty bread.

Bacon

Onion

Carrot

Potatoes

Paprika

Fish stock

Bay leaf

Cream

Fish

Dice a strip or two of bacon. Add it to a Dutch oven set over medium-high heat and sauté with a few handfuls of diced onion, carrot, and potatoes, until the onion has gone translucent. Hit the mixture with some salt, pepper, and a flash of paprika, smoked if you have it. Now add enough fish stock so that the potatoes are almost swimming. Add a bay leaf, lower the heat to a simmer, and let bubble along until the liquid has reduced by a third and the potatoes are tender. Add a splash or two of cream and let it heat and thicken slightly. Now cut some fish into chunks and stir them in gently. Five minutes later: chowder.

### Modifications

If you're not a meat eater, grab some butter instead of bacon (or use both if you're me). If you don't have fish stock, sub white wine or even water. Don't have cream in the fridge? Use milk. If you can find good corn on the cob, slice off the kernels and add them for a fine addition. Or go with a cup of frozen corn.

# Peanut Butter Sandwich with Sriracha and Pickles

Here's a spin on a great old sandwich of the American South: peanut butter and pickle. This is a meal of remarkable intensity—sweet and salty, sour, and soft and crisp. Trust me on this one!

Bread

Peanut butter

Sriracha

Soy sauce

Pickles

Toast the bread before spreading it with peanut butter. Add a zigzag of sriracha for warmth, a tiny drizzle of soy sauce, and sliced pickles for crunch.

**Modifications**

Swap sambal oelek for the sriracha. Or chili crisp!

# Grilled Cheese with Jalapeño, Tomato, and a Fried Egg

Sometimes I get it into my head to make a fancy grilled cheese sandwich. I don't have a recipe because no one really needs a recipe to make grilled cheese sandwiches. You just need desire, and a triangle in your head: salt, crunch, melting ooze. And pickles on the side, if you like.

Cheese

Bread

Jalapeño

Tomato

Butter

Mayonnaise

Egg

Slice some mild Cheddar. Get decent bread, a sliced jalapeño, and the tail end of a beefsteak tomato. Assemble the sandwich while some butter starts to foam in a pan. Swipe the outside of the bread with mayo to encourage a golden crust. Make a sunny-side-up fried egg. Then sizzle-sizzle-flip-flip the sandwich in the pan and top with the fried egg. It's the simplest kind of cooking, and on some nights that's exactly what most of us need. Make grilled cheese!

**Modifications**

Instead of an egg, use some reheated leftover chicken, pork, or steak. Spoon out a little ketchup or gochujang as a dip.

# Taleggio Grilled Cheese with Egg and Honey

Here's my memory of an awesome grilled cheese sandwich I had in San Francisco once, at the chef Chris Cosentino's restaurant, Cockscomb. They used duck eggs at Cockscomb, but a fresh chicken egg will do. This is easy to make.

Taleggio

White bread

Butter

Egg

Honey

Build your sandwich out of taleggio and good white bread, butter it on the outside, and grill it in a cast-iron pan until golden on both sides. (Cover the pan for the first side, for extra melt action.) Meanwhile, fry an egg, sunny-side up, until it's a little lacy on the edges but the yolk hasn't set, and then slide it on top of the sandwich. Drizzle with good honey and finish with a light sprinkle of salt and pepper.

# Tomato Sandwich

One of my favorite hot-weather meals.

Bread

Butter

Mayonnaise

Tomato

Toast and butter your bread. Add a good swipe of mayo. Load up with sliced tomato. Season with a healthy turn of black pepper and a spray of salt.

**Modifications**

The tomatoes are good but not great? A tiny, tiny pinch of sugar on them will help. So will a quickly fried soft-shell crab! You can also add a slab of mozzarella and some torn basil.

# Roasted Mushrooms with Buttered Baguette

Simplicity itself and beyond delicious, even if you aren't able to secure a pound of perfect chanterelles.

Baguette

Butter

Wild mushrooms

Olive oil

Thyme

Parsley

Buy a baguette and some very good butter, along with a pound of wild mushrooms, preferably chanterelles. Clean the mushrooms gently with a damp paper towel, then toss them with olive oil, salt, pepper, and some fresh thyme leaves, if you have them, or a scant scattering of dry if you don't. (If you don't have those either, no worries.) Put the mushrooms on a sheet pan and roast at 375°F for about 15 minutes, or until they've released a fair amount of liquid. Remove the pan from the oven and drain off the liquid into a food storage container. Continue roasting the mushrooms for 25 to 30 minutes longer, or until they're a little crisp on the outside and soft inside and awesome. Cut the baguette and slather with butter. Serve with the mushrooms, scattering some chopped parsley over the top of both, if you have some to spare.

**Tip**

You can use the mushroom liquid to add as a seasoning for soup. Store in the refrigerator for up to a week or in the freezer indefinitely.

# Mushrooms on Toast with Greens and Eggs

Eggs for dinner, on toast, with a mushroom gravy and wilted greens.

Mushrooms

Butter

Cream

Olive oil

Hearty greens

Bread

Eggs

Sauté some sliced mushrooms in butter until they've released their liquid and that liquid is gone. Hit them with salt and pepper and then with enough cream that it can reduce a little, and you'll think of it as gravy. Pour the mushrooms and their sauce into a small bowl and wipe out the pan. Warm some olive oil in it over medium-high heat and toss in a bunch of sturdy greens—some Tuscan kale, for instance—to wilt. Put these greens on a plate next to the bowl of mushroom gravy and return the pan to the heat. Add a splash of olive oil and a pat of butter to melt while you put some bread in the toaster. Crack as many eggs as you need into the fat and cook as you like—I like sunny-side up, with lacy edges. Toast is done. Top it with mushroom gravy, then greens, and then an egg like a hat. Salt and pepper the dish and serve. Very nice!

**Tip**

Baby bella mushrooms are nice here, but the dish is incredible with wild mushrooms, and with chanterelles in particular. Cook a pound of them for every two people served.

**Modifications**

You don't, of course, need the eggs. Nor the greens. You could cook the mushrooms with chopped garlic and thyme. You could use crème fraîche in place of the cream.

# Ham and Radicchio Toast

Stop at the market and pick up a loaf of the best available bread you'd want to eat for dinner—a country loaf of some kind, most probably, or a good baguette. Get a small head of radicchio as well, some hot mustard, and a half pound of thin-sliced ham from the deli counter.

Ham

Radicchio

Olive oil

Good bread

Hot mustard

Slice the ham and radicchio into ribbons, toss the radicchio in a hot sauté pan with a few glugs of olive oil, and sauté until softened. Take the pan off the stove, add the ham, and toss to combine. Meanwhile, slice some bread and toast it perfectly. Then slash a bit of hot mustard onto all the slices. Pile the warm radicchio and ham mixture onto the bread slices. You'll be doing this once or twice a month for a while.

# Italian Subs with Peppers and Sausage

Sometimes a hero is a lot more than a sandwich, particularly on nights when you don't really want to cook but find that once you *are* cooking, all you want is big flavor. Here's an Italian American example.

Onions

Olive oil

Red pepper flakes

Bell peppers

Italian sausages

Sub sandwich rolls

Mozzarella

Slice two big sweet onions and set them in a hot pan with a couple of gurgles of olive oil. Season with salt, pepper, and a shake of red pepper flakes, then cook over medium heat, stirring and tossing occasionally, until they go golden and soft. That'll take a while. Add a couple of sliced bell peppers to the pan and continue cooking, still stirring and tossing, until they begin to wilt. Set the vegetables aside. About halfway through, cook some sweet Italian sausages in another hot, oil-slicked pan until crisp and brown on the exterior, turning often. Split your sub rolls and rip out a little of the interior from each. Load one side of each roll with some of the onions and peppers, the other with a sausage. Top with mozzarella, put the open sandwiches on a sheet pan and slide into a hot oven until the cheese is melted and the bread is lightly toasted. Fold together and serve.

**Tip**

Stick the bits of bread you removed from the sub rolls in a food processor and whir to break down into fresh bread crumbs. Store in the freezer indefinitely.

**Modifications**

Use provolone in place of the mozzarella. Swipe some anchovy-garlic butter (see page 14) onto the toasted hero rolls before serving.

# Crispy Pork Sandwiches with Spicy Mayo and Scallions

This is a rendition of restaurant food, made with supermarket ingredients.

Pork belly or fatty pork chops

Soy sauce

Oyster sauce

Chile oil

Sugar

Hamburger buns

Mayonnaise

Chili-garlic sauce

Scallions

Cilantro

Get some pork belly if you can or some fatty pork chops if you can't. Cut the meat into cubes or planks. Toss those with a mixture of soy sauce and oyster sauce, some hot chile oil, and a sprinkle of sugar. Line a sheet pan with foil and heat your broiler. Cook the pork under the broiler, tossing it around a couple times, until it's crisp, glistening, and cooked all the way through. Toast the buns. Stir together some mayo and chili-garlic sauce. Mix in a lot of sliced scallions and cilantro. Smear the buns with the mayo mixture. Get the pork onto the buns, top with more scallions and cilantro if you like, and there you go.

**Tip**

You can cook the meat on the stove top in a sauté pan, but only if you have a good exhaust fan above your stove. You can make it in a cast-iron skillet set over an outdoor grill as well.

**Modification**

If you don't have hamburger buns, go with toasted English muffins.

# Ham and Brie Sandwich

This is a version of a ham-and-cheese Dagwood that they serve at the Orient Country Store at the far end of Long Island. You can have it for lunch or dinner, but it makes for a stellar breakfast if you lay in the supplies correctly. I like this sandwich for lunch very much.

Ham

Apple

Brie

Dijon mustard

Baguette

Get some thin-sliced deli ham and your favorite variety of apple, along with Brie of the best quality you can manage, a little Dijon, and a baguette. Leave the cheese on the countertop for a while before making, so you can use it to butter the baguette, quite thickly. Then layer less ham than you'd think on top of the cheese, along with a run of thin-sliced apple with a wisp of mustard. It makes for a substantial feed.

**Tip**

If you can manage to warm the baguette before assembling the sandwich, the cheese will take on an extra creaminess that slicks the ham and enhances the sweetness of the apple. No lie.

**Modification**

You can add a fried egg to the situation, if you're hungry or if your work puts you outside and laboring in a physical way.

# Bloody Mary Spiedies

Spiedies are a specialty of upstate New York: tough meat marinated in Italian dressing for a very long time, then grilled crisp and juicy and served with soft bread and hot sauce. Delicious.

A big bloody Mary

Horseradish

Olive oil

Meat

Italian bread

Butter

Perhaps the most amazing spiedies are marinated in a bloody Mary of tomato juice, vodka, salt and pepper, loads of hot sauce, lemon juice, and Worcestershire sauce. Some people will like a punch of garlic, onion powder, and celery seed in their bloody Mary. (Others, a bloody Mary mix.) Whichever, I demand a big hit of horseradish whisked with olive oil. Slide some cubed meat—beef, pork, chicken, lamb, venison—into that and let it sit for a day. Then thread the cubes onto skewers and broil, turning often to crisp and cook through. Serve with grocery-store Italian bread, warmed and buttered.

**Tips**

At some point someone is going to give you a house gift of bloody Mary mix. This is what you're going to do with it. If you can add some freshly grated horseradish, rather than jarred, to the bloody Mary so much the better.

# The Vegetable Aisle

# Corn Salad with Tomato and Arugula

Summer in edible form.

Corn

Tomatoes

Baby salad greens

Olive oil

Lemon or vinegar

Parmesan

Get some fresh corn and cut it off the cob. Combine it with big chunks of the best tomatoes you can find and some baby greens or arugula. That's a salad, when dressed simply with olive oil and a spray of lemon juice or vinegar and a little salt. Shave some Parmesan over the top and add a few grinds of pepper. Hungry cats may grill a couple of sausages and add them to the plate.

# Zucchini Slaw with Yogurt and Herbs

Someone left a lot of zucchini on my counter one time and, after I stared at it a while, I made it into zucchini slaw and served it with a loaf of Italian bread and some scallops quickly sautéed in butter. That's a pretty great meal, in zucchini season.

Zucchini

Lemon

Yogurt

Parsley

Mint

Any seeds or nuts

Parmesan

Thinly slice the zukes and toss them with salt, pepper, and the zest and juice of a lemon. Let sit for a few minutes to cure. Add a scoop of yogurt and stir everything to coat the vegetables. Put some fistfuls of chopped parsley and mint on top, along with a few tablespoons of seeds or nuts. Grate some Parmesan over. That's it!

**Tips**

The only issue you'll have along the way is figuring out how much yogurt to add. The correct amount will dress the zucchini rather than cloak it—think summer shirt, not winter overcoat.

**Modification**

Use yellow straightneck or crookneck summer squash in place of the zucchini, no problem. You could add a little chopped feta, if you have it.

# Brown Butter Tomato Salad

Here's a no-recipe recipe that I hacked out of Gabrielle Hamilton's exquisite and bossy cookbook, *Prune*. Unlike a lot of the no-recipe recipes I favor, this one demands perfect tomatoes, the sort you generally only find for a month or so each year, at the end of the summer, when perfect tomatoes are all you want to eat. Serve with good bread, for mopping up the butter and tomato juices.

Tomatoes

Butter

Cut some tomato beauties into thick planks and arrange them prettily on a platter. Heat some good butter in a pan until it is foamy and just starting to turn nutty and brown, then spoon it all over the tomatoes—neatly, please, as they do at a restaurant. Sprinkle coarse salt over the top for texture. Come winter, you'll try it again with wan tomatoes, and it won't be the same.

# Fried Halloumi with Cucumber Salad

I love my colleagues at The Times for a thousand reasons, but in particular for their occasional enthusiasm for my tradition of cooking without recipes. Julia Moskin gave me a great no-recipe recipe once: fried halloumi, the firm Greek cheese with a high melting point, with a cucumber salad. You'll need enough cheese for at least one thick plank per person.

Cucumber

Tomato

Olive oil

Parsley

Mint

Lemon

Bread or pita

Halloumi

Combine diced cukes and a chopped ripe tomato or two, a lot of olive oil and pepper, and some parsley and mint. Taste and add salt, but not too much because the cheese is salty. Then cut a lemon into wedges to serve on the side, and put some crusty bread or pitas wrapped in foil in a low oven to warm. Meanwhile, cut the cheese into finger-thick slices or sticks. Heat a well-seasoned or nonstick pan, well swirled with olive oil, until it is nearly smoking. Add the halloumi and cook, turning the pieces a few times, until they are golden brown on all sides. Call your people to the table. Everyone gets a slice or two of cheese and a healthy pile of salad. Pass the lemon and bread on the side.

**Modifications**

Mexican queso blanco works well, too, if you can't find halloumi, and so does aged provolone. You can, as always, grill some sausages if you need a little more heft to the meal.

# Kale Salad with Cranberries, Pecans, and Blue Cheese

Kale salads have fallen into disfavor among the cognoscenti because for a while they were on every restaurant menu in town. There was a reason for that though, and this salad shows it plain.

Mustard

Olive oil

Lemon

Kale

Dried cranberries

Toasted pecans

Blue cheese

Croutons

Make a mustardy vinaigrette that'll stand up to the greens: mustard, olive oil, a splash of lemon juice, salt, and pepper. Drizzle it over stemmed and chopped kale with a host of big-flavored mix-ins that wink at whatever season you're in without being dorky about it, which in this case, are dried cranberries plus pecans. And some crumbled blue cheese and a spray of croutons. Sweet, salty, spicy, sour. That and a chilled glass of red wine. Why don't we eat salads for dinner more often?

**Modifications**

Substitute currants for the cranberries. Toss raw pecans with a glug of maple syrup and a dusting of cayenne and then toast for a sweet-spicy lift.

# Roasted Sweet Potato Salad

This is a meal-size salad to remind you of—while being much better than—those free-with-the-sushi specials you were served at the Japanese place you once kind of liked even though it wasn't very good. Sweet potatoes make the difference.

Sweet potatoes

Neutral oil

Miso

Butter

Scallions

Sesame seeds
or furikake
(see page 100)

Peanuts

Garlic

Ginger

Rice vinegar

Sesame oil

Soy sauce

Salad greens

Cut the sweet potatoes in half lengthwise, oil them with canola or grapeseed oil, and then roast them cut-side down in a hot oven until they're soft and cooked through and a little caramelized at the edges. Flip them over and top with a mixture of miso, softened butter, scallions, sesame seeds or furikake, and a handful of chopped roasted peanuts. While the potatoes are roasting, combine a little minced garlic and a lot of minced ginger in a bowl with a few tablespoons of rice vinegar, a glug of sesame oil, and a bunch more canola or grapeseed oil. Emulsify the dressing with a whisk and add a hit of soy sauce. Drizzle over a bowl of salad greens, toss well, and serve the potatoes on top.

**Tips**

Butter and miso is an awesome combination. Try it on baked fish or grilled chicken or sautéed tofu.

**Modification**

Tired of soy sauce? How about a drizzle of honey? You'll figure it out.

# Braised Kale with Paprika

A smoky bowl of braised kale is a fine accompaniment to grilled chicken, but it's equally good alone, atop a bowl of rice.

Olive oil

Onion

Garlic

Tomato paste

Paprika

Vegetable stock or chicken stock

Red wine vinegar

Kale

Red pepper flakes

Place a big heavy-bottomed pot with a lid over medium-high heat and add a few glugs of olive oil. When the oil shimmers, sauté a diced onion and a few cloves of minced garlic until they soften, then hit the mixture with a couple tablespoons of tomato paste and a good, heavy shake of smoked paprika, if you have any, or regular paprika, if you don't. Stir that together and cook until it all begins to darken, then add a couple cups of stock to the mix, along with a splash of red wine vinegar. As it comes to a boil, add as much stemmed and chopped kale as you need to feed your crowd, and cover the pot to steam. Stir the mixture a few times as the greens soften, then season with salt, pepper, and red pepper flakes and serve. Holy moly, it's good.

**Modifications**

You can make the dish with collards, if you like, or any other big, hearty green. If you don't have stock, just use water.

# Broccoli with Ham and Melted Cheese

You'll need only a couple handfuls of broccoli florets per person. Serve over pasta or rice, if you like.

Broccoli

Olive oil

Ham

Cheese

Cook broccoli florets in boiling water just until they're beginning to go soft. Drain. Then heat up a skillet with some olive oil in it. Use it to heat through some chopped ham. When you're ready to eat, add the broccoli to the hot oil and shake it around, then sprinkle shredded Cheddar or Jarlsberg or spoon Brie into the pan—anything that'll melt into unctuousness—and toss it all around over low heat until everything is cloaked in cheese. Grind some pepper over the top, and dinner is served.

**Modifications**

Substitute prosciutto, bacon, or guanciale for the ham. Vegetarian? You don't need the meat. Don't like broccoli? Use cauliflower or green beans.

# Grilled Broccoli with Soy Sauce, Maple Syrup, and Balsamic Vinegar

This is a good no-recipe recipe to have in your back pocket when you're cooking burgers and dogs on the grill. It's a take on a dish that I first learned from the Brooklyn restaurateur Joe Carroll. Never mind burgers or hot dogs or anything else, actually. I could go for this broccoli on white rice and call it dinner, full stop.

Broccoli

Soy sauce

Balsamic vinegar

Maple syrup

Neutral oil

Red pepper flakes

Sesame seeds
or furikake
(see page 100)

Toss broccoli florets in equal parts soy sauce and balsamic vinegar, a generous dash of maple syrup, and a splash of oil, then grill (or broil) until they're caramelized and cooked through. Serve them under a scattering of red pepper flakes and sesame seeds or furikake.

# Miso-Glazed Eggplant with a Bowl of Rice

A simple dinner with a lot of flavor to it.

Rice

Eggplants

Neutral oil

Miso

Sesame oil

Rice wine

Soy sauce

Sesame seeds

You know how to make rice, so make some. For the rest of the dish, grab some small eggplants—the Japanese variety is a good option—and halve and then cut them on the diagonal into little steaks. Drizzle them with neutral oil and roast in a 400°F oven for 20 minutes or so, turning them once or twice, until they're soft. Then crank the oven to broil and paint them with white miso that's been cut with splashes of sesame oil and rice wine, a smaller splash of soy sauce, and a few grinds of pepper. Let that get going until the eggplant skin begins to pop, then serve those little vegetarian flavor steaks over the rice, with a spray of sesame seeds over the top.

**Tip**

Whatever miso you have
is the correct one to use.

# Shaved Cucumbers with Peanut Sauce

I'm no Spiralizer, but this is a fine meal when the weather is hot.

Cucumbers

Peanut butter

Rice vinegar

Soy sauce

Ginger

Garlic

Red pepper flakes

Cilantro

Peanuts

Peel two or three cucumbers, then shave the flesh into ribbons that are like noodles. Dress that "pasta" with a sauce of a spoonful of peanut butter thinned out with a splash of warm water and a few tablespoons of rice vinegar and soy sauce. Add grated ginger, minced garlic, and a pinch of red pepper flakes. Maybe some lime juice? Top the dish with a sprinkling of chopped cilantro and a handful of chopped roasted peanuts. Dinner!

# Asparagus and Boursin Tart

This is the sort of meal that I imagine Robert B. Parker's fictional detective Spenser might make for his lover, Susan Silverman—Boston cosmopolitan cooking circa the early '80s. Nostalgia alert!

Frozen puff pastry

Asparagus

Boursin cheese

Arugula

Herbs

Pull some frozen puff pastry from the freezer and let thaw until it is easily unfolded. Roast or boil a bunch of asparagus. Chop it into bite-size pieces. Roll out the puff pastry on the back of a sheet pan so the rim doesn't get in the way of your rolling pin. Trim ¾-inch strips from all four sides. Press those on top of the pastry along the edges, so you can make a raised border around the perimeter of the tart. Prick the bottom of the pastry and partially bake in a 350°F oven (on the inverted pan) until it's golden and puffy, about 25 minutes. Remove and press down the center a little, to deflate it. Slather with softened Boursin, cover with the asparagus, and return to the oven for 15 minutes or so, then top with torn arugula and chopped herbs. Let's go!

## Tip

Use a butter-based frozen puff pastry, if you can, or one made with vegetable-based fats, if you can't.

## Modifications

Instead of asparagus, cook a bag of frozen peas in butter. Some consider Boursin a processed food and won't abide it. If that's you, try softened cream cheese instead, and fork in some chopped garlic, parsley, and chives.

# Black Bean Tacos

This is a good midweek pantry raid of a dinner and comes together in about 20 minutes. Light work.

Onion

Olive oil

Chile powder

Canned black beans

Lime

Tortillas

Cheese

Crunchy lettuce

Radishes

Sauté a chopped onion in a small pot with some olive oil, then sprinkle with chile powder, salt, and pepper. Add a can of drained black beans and simmer until hot. Drizzle the beans with the juice of a lime and set aside. Serve on warm tortillas with a shower of shredded Cheddar and some chopped lettuce and slices of radish.

# Pizza without a Crust

This is one of those dinners that's pure mess and fun, and all it takes are some canned tomatoes and mozzarella, some of the same toppings you might put on a pie, and a focaccia or loaf of Italian bread from the market.

Canned tomatoes

Olive oil

Garlic

Mozzarella

Bread

Condiments

Put a large can of good tomatoes into a food processor with a couple glugs of olive oil, some salt, and a clove of garlic. Whiz that up and pour it into a deep sauté pan set over medium heat and let it to come to a simmer. Slice or tear your mozzarella into pieces. When the sauce is hot, lay the cheese on top of the liquid and slide the pan into a 400°F oven to get melty and fine. Then serve that in the middle of your table as if it were a fondue, alongside some bread and condiments: olives, say, or anchovies, chopped basil, red pepper flakes, grated Parmesan . . . whatever you like. Dip, eat, repeat.

# The Staples Sisters: Rice and Pasta

# Kitchen-Sink Rice and Beans

Canned beans are a staple of the no-recipe cooking set, an easy way to jump-start a fast and easy dinner, especially if you can layer flavors into them with a sofrito of what's available to you in the fridge. Make these beans out of what you have, and you'll discover the secret truth of improvisatory cooking: it works!

Rice

Bacon

Pickled peppers

Shallots

Garlic

Cilantro

Cumin

Orange juice

Canned beans

Bread

Butter

Hot sauce

Lime

Make a pot of rice. Chop a few strips of bacon and add to a skillet with, say, pickled peppers (I like banana peppers), sliced shallots, chopped garlic, minced cilantro, ground cumin, salt, and a splash of orange juice. Cook down into a kind of syrup. Tip a can or two of beans with their liquid into that—I like black, though red kidney beans are delicious in this as well—then mix and allow the flavors to come together at a slow simmer. Toast and butter the bread. Serve the beans over the rice with hot sauce and a squeeze of lime, accompanied by the buttered toast. Delicious every time.

### Modifications

You can replace the bacon with ground pork or sausage or make it without meat. Use pineapple or mango juice in place of the orange, or no juice at all. You can lose the banana peppers or use jalapeños in place of them, or just load on the hot sauce. Shallots? So fancy. Use an onion instead, or the whites of the scallions from back of the crisper.

# Curried Beans and Rice

One of my kids made this for dinner one night, riffing on what we had in the pantry. There was still some left when her parents got home from the gig that had kept them from feeding their children themselves. They were hungry, and the hugs doled out that night were especially tight. This dish has since joined our starting rotation of family meals.

Rice

Onion

Garlic

Olive oil

Ground pork

Curry powder

Canned black beans

Make rice, as you do. While it's steaming, sauté some chopped onion and garlic in olive oil. Then add some ground pork and brown it. Season the mixture with salt, pepper, and a few hefty tablespoons of hot curry powder. Add a can of black beans with their liquid, then the cooked rice. Stir everything together and feed everyone who's around. Curried beans and rice is *good*.

# Rice and Beans with Extras

Perhaps this evening is calling for simple rice and beans, with limes to squeeze over the plate, and warm tortillas to scoop up the food? I like some pickled jalapeños, cilantro, and hot sauce on there, too, but they're not required.

Rice

Onion

Olive oil

Garlic

Bulk sausage

Cumin

Orange juice

Black beans

Limes

Tortillas

Cook a cup or two of rice as you usually do. As the rice steams away, dice an onion and sweat it in a saucepan with a drizzle or two of olive oil set over medium-high heat. When the onion begins to go translucent, add a few cloves of chopped garlic and some sausage and cook until the meat has started to crisp and the onion has started to caramelize. Add a healthy dusting of ground cumin, sprinkle with some salt and pepper, and allow it all to go muddy and fragrant. Splash the mixture with orange juice, maybe half a cup, and allow it to cook down, almost to syrup. Then add a big can of drained black beans and stir to combine, turning down the heat and allowing the flavors to come together, perhaps using a spoon to mash some of the beans as they cook. Serve it all on top of the finished rice, adorned with wedges of lime and accompanied by warmed tortillas.

**Modifications**

Sub ground beef or ground lamb for the sausage. Or feel free to skip the meat and keep this vegetarian. And if you don't have tortillas, buttered toast will suffice.

The New York Times Cooking No-Recipe Recipes

# Dried Fruit and Almond Pilaf

Here's a free-form rice pilaf, made with onion, dried fruit, and slivered almonds. Serve alongside a store-bought roast chicken, the legs and thighs separated, and the breasts cut on the bias and fanned out for show.

Butter

Onion

Rice

Dried fruit

Slivered almonds

First, melt a knob of butter in a pot, then sauté a sliced onion in it until translucent. Add rice, as much as you want to cook, and stir it around until opaque. Then add water in its usual ratio to the rice, and cook as you always do. At the end, add some chopped prunes, currants, raisins, or all three, along with a handful of slivered almonds, and some salt and pepper. Fluff the rice to mix everything together. Put the top back on the pot and let the rice and mix-ins mellow out for a few minutes.

# Weeknight Fried Rice

It's always good to have some cooked rice hanging around in the refrigerator or freezer, because you can make this dinner with it anytime you like. (Chilling the rice helps separate the grains during stir-frying.)

Cooked rice

Frozen diced vegetables

Any meat or tofu

Eggs

Garlic

Ginger

Scallions

Soy sauce

Sesame oil

Gochujang

Neutral oil

Start with cooked rice, white or brown, a cup or so per person, made fresh and chilled or pulled from the freezer, where you keep some in a plastic bag against the promise of just such an exercise. Also helpful, also in the freezer: bags of diced organic vegetables you can get at the market (the mixed corn, carrots, and peas number, for instance). For the rest, assemble meat, if you eat meat, or tofu; a couple of whisked eggs; about a tablespoon each of minced garlic and ginger; and some scallions. You can make a sauce from soy sauce and sesame oil (about a 3:1 ratio) and fire it up with a teaspoon or two of gochujang. You'll need a little less than a quarter cup of sauce to cook for four.

To the wok! Crank the heat, add a little oil, and toss in a handful of chopped meat or tofu. After it crisps, fish it from the pan and set on a plate. Add the garlic and ginger and a handful of chopped scallions. Stir-fry for 30 seconds or so, then add those frozen vegetables. More stir-frying. Return the meat to the wok. Stir-fry. Clear a space in the center of the wok and add the eggs, cooking them quickly to softness. Throw in the sauce, then the rice, and mix it all together until it's steaming hot. Finish with more chopped scallions.

# Ketchup and Kimchi Fried Rice

Here's an easy fried-rice dinner made in the spirit of the Los Angeles chef Roy Choi, with ketchup and kimchi from the jar in the back of the fridge.

Neutral oil

Scallions

Carrots

Garlic

Kimchi

Cooked, chilled white rice

Ketchup

Soy sauce

Eggs

Add a bit of oil to a hot wok and stir-fry thinly sliced scallions, carrots, garlic, and kimchi. Then add a couple cups of leftover white rice and fry until crisp. Hit that mixture with some ketchup and a splash of soy sauce and stir to combine. Crack a couple eggs into a bowl and break up with a fork. Open a hole in the middle of the wok and tip the eggs into it. Mix to cook the eggs and combine everything once more. That's dinner right there and, soon, again another night.

# Sautéed Greens with Soy Sauce Rice and Furikake

An afternoon snack for some, but I find steamed rice served with a drizzle of soy sauce and a pat of butter a delicious plain dinner. Improving on the original, see if you can lay your hands on some furikake, the dry Japanese seasoning made with ground dried fish, sesame seeds, chopped dried seaweed, a little sugar, a little salt, and probably some monosodium glutamate. It's so much better with that pop of flavor and crunch of texture.

Rice

Hearty greens

Garlic

Ginger

Neutral oil

Oyster sauce

Rice vinegar

Soy sauce

Furikake

Make your rice. Sauté a tangle of greens with minced garlic and ginger in some oil, then hit them with a loose drizzle of oyster sauce cut with rice vinegar and a splash of soy sauce. Serve over the rice and sprinkle furikake over the top.

# Pot Stickers with Tomato Sauce

You absolutely do not need a recipe, ever, to cook with inexpensive Chinese, Japanese, or Korean frozen dumplings (often labeled "pot stickers"). But I learned to cook them better after I read the blogger and author Mandy Lee's exhortation to combine them with an Italian-ish tomato sauce, in her wondrous-strange cookbook *The Art of Escapism Cooking*.

Canned tomatoes

Garlic

Thyme

Red pepper flakes

Fish sauce

Brown sugar

Frozen dumplings

Cream

Parmesan

Olive oil

Puree a can of tomatoes with garlic, thyme, red pepper flakes, a big splash of fish sauce, and a spoonful of brown sugar. Simmer that in a skillet until it thickens, then add dumplings of whatever style, straight from the freezer, and let them cook through in the sauce, stirring gently so they don't actually pot-stick. Stir in a little cream at the end and serve with grated Parmesan and a drizzle of olive oil. Kooky fantastic!

## Tips

Supermarket pot stickers are typically filled with pork, chicken, shrimp, and/or vegetables. I've found the chicken and vegetable ones to be substandard for this recipe, but the pork is excellent and the shrimp divine.

## Modifications

No fish sauce on hand? Just omit or add a couple of anchovies to the pan in its place. They'll collapse in the heat. Add a few cubes of mozzarella at the end for extra comfort.

# Soba Noodles with Tofu and Kimchi

I like this dinner so much, sometimes with roasted asparagus on top or a soft-boiled egg. And it's super-simple.

Garlic

Ginger

Soy sauce

Hoisin sauce

Maple syrup

Sesame oil

Red pepper flakes

Tofu

Neutral oil

Soba noodles

Kimchi

Using a large wide serving bowl, make a sauce of minced garlic and ginger, some soy sauce, a spoonful of hoisin sauce, a splash of maple syrup, another of sesame oil, and a lot of red pepper flakes and whisk it all together. Set aside a couple tablespoons of the sauce. Cut the tofu into manageable pieces and pat very dry with a towel. Heat a good quantity of canola or other neutral oil in a big sauté pan, then add the tofu in a single layer and fry it over medium-high heat, turning to brown every side. Cook the soba in boiling water as you fry. When the tofu is done, toss it, carefully, with the sauce in the serving bowl. Drain the soba and then arrange it in the bowl, with the soba to one side of the tofu and the kimchi to the other side. Drizzle with the reserved sauce. You're welcome.

### Modifications

To add soft-boiled eggs to the meal, see instructions on page 14. If you don't have hoisin, sub oyster sauce. Roast asparagus in a very hot oven, tossing every few minutes, until the stalks are tender-crisp. Or grill them! Cut into bite-size lengths and add to the bowl, tucked in alongside the kimchi.

# Instant Ramen, Back-of-the-Fridge Style

It's easier than you might think to transform one of those instant ramen packages from the pantry into something delicious. Just look in the refrigerator for inspiration.

Instant ramen

Stuff from the fridge

Prepare the ramen as directed. But you might stir a single egg per person into the soup for egg-drop glory, cover the surface with chopped fresh mint and cilantro, and then drizzle with sesame oil. Or you could add a tangle of greens, minced garlic, and a gloop of oyster sauce. You could do all of the above. These punch-ups transform a grim dorm-room mealtime into something rather more glamorous and enjoyable. That's what we're looking for sometimes, particularly when cooking is the last thing we want to do.

# Cheese Ravioli with Duck Liver Mousse Sauce

It used to be you had to go to a fancy supermarket if you wanted to buy fresh ravioli or a little tub of duck liver mousse. Now you can score those ingredients at the big box in rural Florida and at the chain shop in North Dakota. Serve with a big green salad and plenty of bread to mop up the sauce.

Red onion

Butter

Capers

Red pepper flakes

Duck liver mousse

Cheese ravioli

Parmesan

Put a big pot of salted water on the stove and set it to boil. Gently sauté a diced small red onion in a huge amount of unsalted butter, then add a handful of capers and a few shakes of red pepper flakes and let it get hot. Tip the tub of mousse into the onion and capers, and let it melt into a sort of buttery paste. Cook the ravioli in the boiling water. Just before pulling them out, ladle a half cup or so of the pasta water into the sauce, which will loosen it up nicely. Pour it into a high-sided serving dish and place the ravioli on top. Serve it all under a shower of grated Parmesan. Oh, wow.

**Tip**

Always salt your pasta cooking water. It adds flavor to the pasta. Make it as salty as the sea.

# Pasta with Garbanzos and a Negroni

Need a dinner plan? Make a Negroni, then pasta with garbanzos and tomato sauce.

Gin

Sweet vermouth

Campari

Orange peel

Onion

Olive oil

Garlic

Tomato paste

Canned tomatoes

Cinnamon

Cream

Pasta

Canned garbanzos

Parsley

Red pepper flakes

First, the Negroni: Mix one part gin, one part sweet vermouth, and one part Campari. Stir with ice, strain over ice, and garnish with orange peel. Sip! Next, chop an onion and sauté it in olive oil with a few minced garlic cloves and a spray of salt and pepper. Have another hit of Negroni. When the mixture has just started to brown, add a tablespoon of tomato paste and a large can of diced tomatoes, along with a stick of cinnamon or a few shakes of ground cinnamon. Stir and simmer away for 10 minutes or so, or longer if you can wait, then add enough cream so that the sauce turns softer in color, running pink. Meanwhile, boil salted water and cook your favorite pasta (I like orecchiette for this) until it is just al dente. Drain, toss in a can of drained garbanzos, and stir the whole thing into the tomato sauce, topping with chopped parsley and a sprinkle of red pepper flakes. Finish that Negroni. Eat.

### Modifications

Don't have cream? Use half-and-half. If you have only canned whole tomatoes, just break them up with the back of a spoon.

# Pasta with Sausage and Sage

Let's say you have some pasta shells in the larder, or orecchiette, or penne, or ziti, or tagliatelle, and you can lay hands on a bunch of spicy Italian sausage, some butter, and a fistful of sage. Get some water going on the stove for the pasta, and you'll have dinner in an instant.

Italian sausages

Olive oil

Butter

Pasta

Sage

Parmesan

Sear the sausages, tucked tightly in a pan with some olive oil. Cut into coins and then fry again in a lot of foaming butter that turns brown in the heat. Boil salted water and cook your favorite pasta until it is just al dente. Drain. Stir dried or minced fresh sage into the sausage just before you tip in the pasta. Stir everything around under a shower of grated Parmesan. I'm telling you true; you should give this a try.

## Modifications

You needn't use spicy Italian sausage if sweet is more your style, and, of course, you can use bulk sausage in place of the coins, if coined sausage reminds you too much of the bad pizzeria in town. Add a few handfuls of greens to the sauce before you add the sage and toss with the pasta. It's a terrific way of bringing greens to the table without the bother of making a separate side dish or salad.

# Amatriciana on the Fly

Here's a half-hour challenge that's no challenge at all. Serve with red pepper flakes and extra cheese on the side.

Bacon

Olive oil

Onion

Pasta

Canned tomatoes

Butter

Pecorino romano

Parsley

Set a large pot of salted water on the stove over high heat. In a pan, sauté chopped bacon—slab bacon, if you can get it—in a glug or two of olive oil until it's crisp. Using a slotted spoon, remove the bacon and place on a paper towel–lined plate to drain. Add chopped onion to the fat, cooking until it's soft and fragrant. Meanwhile, cook enough pasta to feed your crowd until it is just shy of tender. While it cooks, add some canned crushed tomatoes and the cooked bacon to the onion, and stir it to make a sauce. Drain the pasta, then toss it with a knob of butter, and add the pasta to the sauce. Slide all that into a warm serving bowl, then top with grated pecorino. A scattering of chopped parsley adds a festive, poinsettia-and-holly feel, but you can omit it if the clock's ticking.

**Tip**

Figure one slice of bacon and half an onion per person.

The New York Times Cooking No-Recipe Recipes

# Pasta Puttanesca

Make this free-form puttanesca a few times and watch your kitchen confidence soar. Serve it over linguine or spaghetti or bucatini or whatever dried pasta you happen to have in the house. I like it with shells sometimes, because the olives can get lost in them.

Anchovies

Garlic

Olive oil

Pasta

Canned tomatoes

Olives

Capers

Red pepper flakes

Parmesan

Sauté some anchovies and a lot of minced garlic in a lot of olive oil while your salted pasta water comes to a boil in a big pot. (How many anchovies? How many you got? I go for a minimum of four, and the same with cloves of garlic.) Add your pasta to the pot. When the fish are melted and the garlic's gone gold, add a large can of tomatoes and stir everything together. Let that simmer a while, and get a little thicker, then add the olives and capers, and red pepper flakes until it's as fiery as you like. Taste for salt and pepper. Keep simmering and, when the pasta is done to your liking, taste the sauce again, drain the pasta, and toss it with the sauce. Shower the dish with grated Parmesan and serve.

**Tip**

You can cook the dried pasta directly in the sauce if you like, adding a couple cups of water or chicken stock and covering the pan for 10 minutes or so, stirring occasionally.

# Pasta with Blue Cheese and Walnuts

The difference between me and my colleague Melissa Clark? I find recipes in restaurants and cookbooks, in the kitchens of others. Melissa does that, too, of course. But she can also find deliciousness in her head. Example #1,167 of that: this no-recipe recipe she taught me, for pasta with blue cheese and walnuts.

Pasta

Butter

Blue cheese

Toasted walnuts

Extra virgin olive oil

It's simple: Cook whatever pasta you wish to eat in well-salted water, then save some of the water when you drain it off. Toss the cooked pasta in a warm bowl with a pat or two of unsalted butter, a handful of crumbled blue cheese, and an equal amount of chopped walnuts. Add some of that reserved cooking water and stir it around to make a kind of sauce. Then shower the bowl with pepper and a drizzle of extra-virgin olive oil. Dinner is served.

# Spicy Caper and Olive Pasta

How it happened: There were some capers in the refrigerator and a few olives as well. The kids wanted pasta, so I figured I could chop those up and put them in tomato sauce for puttanesca on the fly. I had no anchovies, though, and no garlic either. It was a really good dinner.

Capers

Olives

Chili-garlic sauce

Fish sauce

Tomato paste

Canned tomatoes

Pasta

Sauté a handful of capers and olives with chili-garlic sauce, then hit the mixture with a splash of fish sauce and a big squeeze of double-strength tomato paste from the tube. Add a large can of tomatoes and let everything simmer, simmer, simmer until the kids bark. Get a pot of water boiling, get the pasta into it, and cook just until al dente. Drain the pasta, dress it with the sauce, and serve it with forks and spoons.

**Modifications**

I used Vietnamese fish sauce because that was what I had, and I liked how it worked. But you could, of course, use colatura di alici, Italian fermented anchovy drippings, instead. Or just a couple of anchovies, cooked until they melt. You should not follow my example and ever allow your pantry to be without them.

# Speedy Sunday Gravy with Ziti

I'm not serving this to your nonna, but on a Thursday night it's about the greatest thing imaginable. Grate some Parmesan over the top, and you've got dinner in about 30 minutes.

Italian sausage

Olive oil

Onion

Garlic

Carrot

Red pepper flakes

Canned tomatoes

Cinnamon

Ziti

Parmesan

Chop some Italian sausage coarsely and add it to a hot pan dressed in a few glugs of olive oil. Cook the meat until it begins to brown, stirring often, and then add a chopped onion, a few cloves of minced garlic, and a diced carrot. Continue to cook, stirring occasionally, until the onion is translucent. Hit the mixture with some salt and pepper, a dash of red pepper flakes, and then add a large can of tomatoes and a cinnamon stick or a pinch of ground cinnamon and stir. Lower the heat and allow all those flavors to come together. Bring a pot of salted water to a boil and cook some ziti until it's just al dente, then add it to the gravy. Rain grated parm over the top. Serve with extra cheese and red pepper flakes on the side.

# Ham and Cheese Pasta Shells with a Handful of Peas

Pick up a box of large shells—the ones the size of a knuckle, so they hold a little sauce in them. Pick up a ham steak from the butcher or the supermarket meat display. Pick up a bag of frozen organic peas as well—they're sweeter than the standard issue. You'll need a block of good Swiss if you can find it, or some Jarlsberg if you can't. (Hey, Jarlsberg melts like a dream.)

Pasta shells

Ham

Butter

Swiss cheese

Peas

Parmesan

Set a large pot of salted water to boil and add your pasta. While the pasta cooks, cube the ham, and get to work on the next burner, browning the ham in a pat of good unsalted butter in a skillet. Offstage, grate about a cup of Swiss cheese into a large serving bowl. When the pasta has been cooked just shy of the time called for on its packaging, throw in a handful of peas, cook another minute, and then drain, reserving a little cooking water. Toss the whole mess into the Swiss cheese, along with the hot ham, another pat or two of butter, and a splash of the pasta water. Watch as the cheese goes soft and ribbony in the heat, and the fat of the ham mingles with the butter and pasta water, and the shells pick up some of it and grab peas in their valves. Shave some Parmesan over the top. Finish with a little pepper. Don't you want to eat that right now?

# Fettuccine with Ricotta and a Fistful of Mint

This is easy elegance for a weeknight and a fearsomely good weekend lunch as well.

Fettuccine

Mint

Shallot

Ricotta

Extra-virgin olive oil

Lemon

Red pepper flakes

Set a pot of nicely salted water over high heat to boil. When it does, add the fettuccine, then get the rest of your dinner ready as it cooks to just al dente. Chop up a fistful of mint and a small shallot. Mix them into a cup or two of fresh ricotta, then loosen the mixture with a healthy drizzle of extra-virgin olive oil and a squeeze of lemon juice. Add some salt and pepper, and a shake of red pepper flakes. When the pasta's done, which'll be about the same time as you're done with the sauce, drain it in a colander and add it to a big warm bowl. Fold the cheese into it, mixing gently. Serve to adoration.

**Modification**

Don't have a shallot? Grab a small onion.

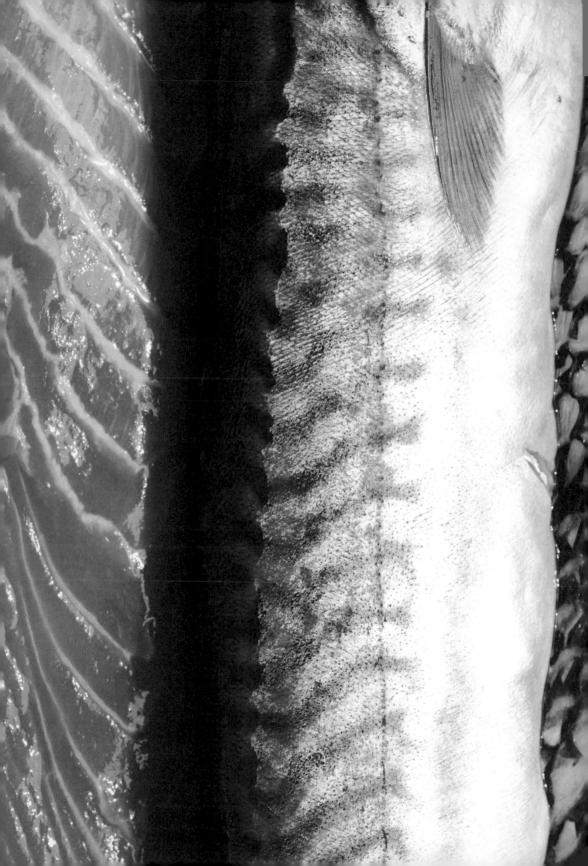

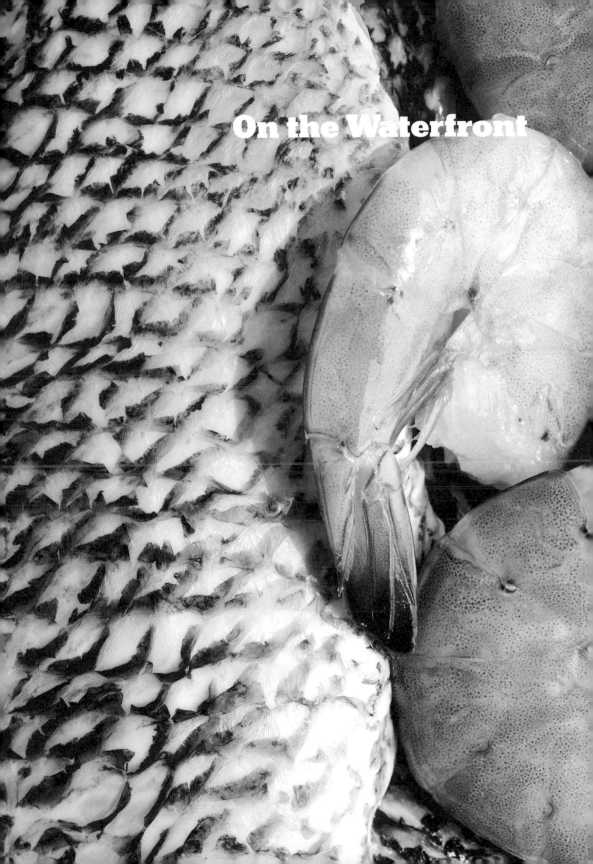

On the Waterfront

# Salt and Pepper Shrimp

The hardest part of making this meal happens before you cook. You need to find the shrimp: ideally, ethically harvested, wild, probably American, flash-frozen.

Shrimp

Neutral oil

Cornstarch

Cilantro

Gently thaw the shrimp in a clean sink filled with cool water, then split the backs and devein them, leaving the shells on. Heat about a cup of oil in a wok until it is almost smoking. Meanwhile, for every half pound of shrimp you've got, figure about a tablespoon of cornstarch and half of that for salt and pepper. Mix the dry ingredients together, and toss with the shrimp. Fry them in the hot oil in a couple of batches, if necessary, until they are pink-gold, crisp at the edges, and just cooked through. Transfer to a platter, sprinkle with a little more salt and chopped cilantro, and serve. Finger food!

**Tip**

A wide sauté pan works just as well, sometimes better, than a wok for this because it offers more surface area for the oil. But I find something delicious about the flavor of shrimp tossed in and out of the oil, and how the shells caramelize against the sides of the wok.

**Modifications**

Of course, you can make this dish with farmed shrimp. I have ethical concerns about that and environmental ones, too. But make your own decisions, always. If you have Sichuan peppercorns to add to the cornstarch mix, great; I like using half a tablespoon of them, toasted in a skillet for a few minutes and then coarsely ground.

# Roasted Shrimp Tacos with Cumin and Chile

Let's say you come across some fat and glistening shrimp, wild-caught, sustainable, beautifully frozen at sea, then thawed at the fishmonger's. Here's what you do next.

Shrimp

Limes

Neutral oil

Cumin

Chile powder

Red pepper flakes

Tortillas

Sour cream

Hot sauce

Cabbage

Toss a whole mess of peeled and deveined shrimp with lime juice and canola oil, and some shakes of ground cumin, chile powder, and red pepper flakes. Then roast them on a sheet pan in a very hot oven alongside a foil-wrapped packet of tortillas. Shouldn't take much more than 8 minutes. Serve the shrimp with sour cream cut with hot sauce and lime juice, shredded cabbage, and more hot sauce, all wrapped in the hot tortillas, with a bunch of lime wedges on the side.

**Tip**

For a cup of sour cream, add the juice of a lime and as much hot sauce as you like. Use as a condiment or as a dressing for shredded cabbage, or both.

**Modification**

I generally use corn tortillas for this recipe, but flour works wonderfully as well.

# Barbecued Shrimp, New Orleans Style

In New Orleans, barbecued shrimp aren't cooked on a grill (or smoked). They're sautéed with salt and pepper, then tossed in butter-mounted Worcestershire sauce with lemon, and sometimes with a splash of cream. Rice, green beans, and plenty of good, crusty bread for mopping up make it an ambrosial meal.

Shallots

Butter

Worcestershire sauce

Thyme

Paprika

Cayenne

Cream

Shrimp

Crank the oven to 450°F and make the sauce on the stove top: Sauté diced shallots in butter, a healthy quarter cup or so of Worcestershire, a little fresh or dried thyme, paprika, cayenne, some salt and pepper, and then a whole lot more butter, cut into the pan a knob at a time and whisked into velvet. Add to that a splash of cream and a few more healthy cranks of pepper. Then roast the deveined shrimp on a greased pan in the oven under a shower of salt and yet more pepper. Serve it on a warm platter with the sauce spooned over the top.

# Seared Scallops with Parsley Salad

Simple, delicious, fast. Maybe serve some toast on the side? I like to have a little crunch from the bread, just for contrast.

Parsley

Shallot

Olive oil

Lemon

Scallops

Butter, bacon fat, or duck fat

Make a salad of chopped parsley, sliced shallot, a little olive oil, a lot of lemon juice, and a sprinkle of salt. Then take your scallops, fat as field mice, and pull and discard the little tabs of muscle from their sides. Put a honking big pat of butter or a spoonful of bacon or duck fat into a large pan set over high heat and sear the scallops hard on one side, then turn them carefully and heat through. Serve on or next to the parsley salad.

**Tip**

If you're lucky enough to live in the Northeast, October and November generally bring bay scallops to market, sweet and small, roughly the size of the end of your pinkie finger. They're fantastic for this dish, but do not cook them as I instruct for regular scallops, searing them hard on one side. You'll overcook a bay scallop that way. Simply warm them through in hot butter and serve.

# Miso-Glazed Scallops

Here's some inspiration for those days when you see fat, super-fresh scallops at the market—day-boat scallops, as they're often called in the Northeast. Serve these with steamed greens and rice.

White miso

Mirin

Scallops

Scallions

Sesame seeds

Mix together a few tablespoons of miso and mirin so that you like the taste. Brush the mixture on scallops that you've either threaded onto a skewer to grill or placed on an oiled sheet pan to run under the broiler for a few minutes. They'll cook fast and brown easily, aided by the sugar in the mirin. Top them with sliced scallions and some sesame seeds. Candy for dinner.

# Steamed Mussels with Tomatoes and Chorizo

Simplicity itself, if you can find a bag of mussels at the store.

Mussels

Cured, dried
Spanish chorizo

Olive oil

Cherry tomatoes

Garlic

White wine

Bread

Parsley

Scrub and debeard the mussel shells as necessary. Then grab a big pot and use it to sauté some cubed chorizo in olive oil over medium-high heat. When it starts to crisp, add a few handfuls of halved cherry tomatoes and a clove or two of chopped garlic. Let the tomatoes blister in the fat, then add the mussels and a glass of white wine. Cover the pot and allow the mussels to steam open. (If at the end you have mussels that haven't opened, ditch them.) Toast some fat slices of bread. Garnish the mussels with chopped parsley and serve with the broth and plenty of toast for the sopping.

# Steamed Clams

Make this once to start off a dinner, and you'll do it often. When I used to keep track of such things, I was easily cooking 1,000 clams a year.

Clams

Garlic

Butter or olive oil

Red pepper flakes

White wine or beer

Bread

Clean your clams well under running water, then sauté some garlic in butter or olive oil in the bottom of a deep pot with a lid. When the garlic is fragrant and soft, add a shake of red pepper flakes to the pot, along with a few healthy glugs of white wine or beer, and then the clams and the lid. Even a scant amount of liquid in the bottom will create the steam necessary to open the clams and release their liquid. (But if you're nervous, add a little water to the alcohol at the start.) Cook the clams until they open, then transfer them to a warm bowl and serve with melted butter and a lot of crusty bread to sop up the broth. You can drink that stuff like soup, like it's bone broth from the sea. It imparts strength and resilience.

**Tip**

When cooled, the clam broth is an excellent addition to a bloody Mary.

**Modification**

Here's a simple dipping sauce for steamed clams, mussels, or to spoon over oven-roasted fish: jalapeño brown butter. Melt butter over medium heat, then add a diced jalapeño, swirling the pan until the foam subsides and the butter turns a deep nut brown. You could drizzle it over a mitten and eat very well.

# Crab Rangoon Burgers

Crab Rangoon—fried dumplings filled with crab-flecked cream cheese—is an appetizer you'll find on the menus of Chinese restaurants across America. At Block16, Paul and Jessica Urban's excellent burger emporium in Omaha, Nebraska, you can find that filling spread on their 3 Happiness Burger, with stir-fried coleslaw and chili-garlic sauce. It is shockingly delicious even if you are not inebriated and is easily made at home. I am serious about this burger, because eating it makes me laugh with delight. But if a burger covered in crab-flavored cream cheese isn't quite your thing, I get it. As the Nebraska tourism board says about Nebraska itself, "Honestly, it's not for everyone."

Canned crab

Cream cheese

Worcestershire sauce

Soy sauce

Mayonnaise

Burger patties

Neutral oil

Burger buns

Cabbage

Hot sauce

All you need to do is flake a can of supermarket crabmeat into a bowl with a brick of softened cream cheese, then thin it out with a little Worcestershire and soy sauce, and maybe a blob of mayo, and mix until it tastes just right. Cook your burger patties, smashed on a hot, oil-slicked cast-iron pan. Toast the buns. Use the crab mixture as a generous topping for the burgers, along with a pile of chopped cabbage and a dash of hot sauce.

**Tip**

You're making a smash burger here, which is thin and crusty when cooked. Don't use more than a couple ounces of meat per burger. You won't be sorry.

# Crisp Fish Fillets with Delicious Sauce

Here's an elegant dinner to adapt to whatever flavors you like. I use stout fillets of whatever white fish I can find and serve them with rice.

Fish fillets

Egg whites

Rice wine

Cornstarch

Sesame oil

Oyster sauce

Soy sauce

Fish sauce

Ginger

Garlic

Neutral oil

Cilantro

Scallions

Aggressively season some fish fillets with salt and pepper, then dip them into a marinade of egg white and rice wine, a spoonful of cornstarch, and a dash of sesame oil. Heat some oyster sauce cut with soy sauce and a little fish sauce, along with some grated ginger and garlic and a splash of water. Fry those fillets in a shallow bath of hot neutral oil. When the fish is crisp and cooked through, put it on a platter and drizzle the warm sauce over it, extravagantly. Finish the whole thing off with chopped cilantro and scallions.

**Modifications**

Instead of oyster sauce and fish sauce, you can make the sauce with soy sauce and melted butter. Or with gochujang, soy sauce, and sesame oil. It's your meal.

# Cod Cakes with Greens

Here's a taste of my childhood, and one of the great ways to cook fish.

Cod

Bay leaf

Lemon

Onion or leek

Olive oil

Garlic

Celery

Mayonnaise

Mustard

Egg

Hot sauce

Parsley

Unsalted Saltines

Neutral oil

Salad greens

Poach a big fillet of cod in water with three or four peppercorns, a bay leaf, and a slice of lemon. Pull the fish from its bath when it has just begun to whiten all the way through, and let it cool. Then sauté a small chopped onion or the white end of a leek (or both) in olive oil, along with a chopped clove of garlic and a handful of diced celery. Allow it, too, to cool. Mix together a generous spoonful of mayo, a smaller one of mustard, an egg, a few dashes of hot sauce, some salt and pepper, and a handful of chopped parsley. Add a cup or so of crushed unsalted Saltines. Add the sautéed vegetables to this mixture and stir to combine. You want the mixture to be pretty loose—add an extra egg if needed to bring it together. Flake the cod into the binding sauce carefully, keeping the pieces as whole as you can manage, then gather the mixture into small balls and form them into little patties. Let these set in the refrigerator on a plate for 20 minutes or so. Fry the patties in a sauté pan, in shimmering-hot neutral oil, such as canola. Serve with the greens, dressed lightly in lemon juice, olive oil, salt, and pepper.

**Tip**

A small smear of mayo on the exterior of the patties before frying will give them a crazy-crisp crust.

**Modifications**

If you don't have Saltines, go with dried bread crumbs (see page 48).

The New York Times Cooking No-Recipe Recipes

# Roasted Fish with Soy, Ginger, and Scallions

Buy a few fillets of the white-fleshed fish you like best (I like fluke). Serve with rice and greens. And I bet any leftovers would make a good sandwich.

Soy sauce

Rice wine or dry sherry

Ginger

Scallions

Fish fillets

Neutral oil

Put a sheet pan in a 425°F oven and let it get hot. Make a sauce in a small bowl: Stir together a few tablespoons of soy sauce for every tablespoon of rice wine or dry sherry, a heap of minced or grated ginger, and plenty of thinly sliced scallions. You could put some garlic in there, if you like, and a dash of hot chili oil or sesame oil. Salt and pepper the fish. Pull the hot sheet pan out of the oven and get some oil on it. Add the fish to the hot pan carefully, put it in the oven, and roast for a minute or so, then paint the sauce onto the fillets and cook for a minute or so longer, until the fish has just cooked through.

# Broiled Fish with Mayo and Mustard

This is an old-school fisherman's preparation, particularly nice with sea bass, salmon, tautog, or grouper. Serve with steamed greens and rice.

Mustard

Mayonnaise

Fish fillets

Simply combine a tablespoon or two of good mustard with an equal amount of mayo, then spread the mixture all over the fish you're cooking. Grind some pepper over the top and put the fish under the broiler or in a hot oven until the topping is bubbling and browned in spots and the fish is cooked through. Should be 5 to 6 minutes, depending on the thickness of the fish.

# Roasted Salmon with Tamari and Lemon

This is my friend Vey's preparation of simple broiled salmon, bathed in tamari and lemon, which she serves with wild rice and buttery steamed broccoli. You can sub in a different rice for the wild rice, or a different vegetable. Add a salad and some bread.

Salmon fillets

Lemon

Neutral oil

Tamari or soy sauce

Marinate some salmon fillets in the juice of a lemon, a good big splash of oil, and the same amount of tamari, which is a little thicker and less salty than soy sauce and is gluten-free. (I like this dish with mushroom soy sauce at that.) Leave your fillets in that mixture while you get the rest of the meal ready. Then, heat your broiler on high. Put the salmon skin-down on a sheet pan covered with oiled foil, perhaps accompanied by some slices of lemon. Slide the pan under the broiler and cook the fish for about 6 minutes, basting it every 2 minutes with the marinade. The result is ambrosial.

**Tip**

Atlantic salmon is considerably cheaper than Pacific salmon. That's because Atlantic salmon is farmed, and much of the Pacific variety is wild, and the economies of scale make it easier to sell farmed fish at a lower price. But I think there is no comparison between their flavor, not to mention the health of the fish or the fishery. I spring for the wild every time.

# Roasted Salmon Fillets with Butter and Soy

Butter and soy sauce are a power couple in matters of flavor and pop, and they play brilliantly with the fatty sweetness of salmon, particularly wild salmon. Serve with mashed potatoes or rice.

Butter

Salmon fillets

Soy sauce

Red pepper flakes

Lemon

Get your oven to 275°F. Smear unsalted butter on a sheet pan, place a couple of fillets of salmon on top, skin-side down, and gently bake the fish for about 20 minutes. When the fillets are done, hit them with some salt and a couple grinds of pepper, a splash of soy, and a scattering of red pepper flakes. Serve with wedges of lemon.

# Salmon with Barbecue Sauce and Hot Peppers

There are generally a few kinds of barbecue sauce in my refrigerator—leftovers from various experiments. That may be true for you as well. I bet there's a half bottle of store-bought sauce in there, or a dusty unopened one in the pantry. Found it? Let's make dinner.

Barbecue sauce

Pickled hot peppers

Butter

Salmon fillets

Neutral oil

Put a good amount of barbecue sauce in a small pot on the stove over medium heat, then turn the oven to 400°F. Coarsely chop a few jarred pickled hot peppers and add to the sauce. Then add a couple pats of butter to silkify the situation. Warm that through while the oven heats. Salt and pepper the salmon fillets and roast them, skin-side down, on a lightly oiled sheet pan for 10 to 12 minutes, or until they are just barely cooked through. Spoon the pepper-studded barbecue sauce over the top. Go to it.

# Teriyaki Salmon with Mixed Greens

Of course, this isn't *real* teriyaki but it's still powerfully good. It just evokes the flavors, in the way a color field on a wall can remind you of France or New England. Serve rice on the side.

Salmon fillets

Soy sauce

Mirin

Garlic

Ginger

Neutral oil

Salad greens

Turn your oven to 400°F or so. While it heats, make a teriyaki sauce with soy sauce cut with mirin, plus a healthy scattering of minced garlic and ginger. It should be salty-sweet. Then put your salmon fillets on a lightly oiled, foil-lined baking sheet, skin-side down. Paint them with the sauce and roast them in the top of the oven for 10 to 12 minutes, painting them again with the sauce at least once along the way. Slide the finished salmon onto piles of mixed greens and drizzle with the remaining sauce. Cooking's not difficult. It just takes practice.

**Tip**

Serve with wedges of lemon, if you have any on hand.

**Modification**

If you don't have mirin, mix brown sugar and a little water.

# Chickens and a Duck

# Rotisserie Chicken Salad

Pick up a heat-lamp roast chicken at the market sometime when you don't want to cook too much. It's okay!

Rotisserie chicken

Baby arugula or other salad greens

Scallions

Cilantro

Avocado

Lime

Garlic

Olive oil

Tear the rotisserie chicken apart to feed four, or use half of it for two, shredding the meat with your fingers. Mix the chicken with a few handfuls of greens, a large handful of sliced scallions, and a lot of chopped cilantro. Cut an avocado or two into the mix. Then make a dressing out of lime juice—one juicy squeezed lime will do—a pressed garlic clove, and a few glugs of olive oil. Season with salt and pepper. Drizzle that over the top and serve. Dinner in 15 minutes, tops.

# Rotisserie Chicken Panzanella

Another thing you can do with a super-tanned heat-lamp chicken from the store.

Rotisserie chicken

Tomatoes

Olive oil

Red wine vinegar

Watercress

Jumbo croutons

Tear a rotisserie chicken into strips and pieces, then cut a few smallish supermarket tomatoes (or better ones, if you've got them) into wedges and marinate them in olive oil, salt, pepper, and red wine vinegar. Pay a few bills or fold some laundry, then turn the whole thing into panzanella by mixing together the chicken, tomatoes, some watercress, and several handfuls of croutons. Shower the salad with pepper and add a spray of salt. This, too, is "cooking."

**Modification**

If you don't have croutons, just cut some stale bread into chunks and toast in a medium oven for about 10 minutes. Or toast fresh bread and tear into hunks.

# Easiest Chicken Teriyaki

You don't need a proper teriyaki sauce to make chicken teriyaki, and you needn't marinate the chicken in it for hours and hours. Just go fast and joyful.

Rice

Soy sauce

Brown sugar

Garlic

Ginger

Cinnamon

Chicken thighs

Scallions

Sesame seeds

Set a pot of rice cooking. Combine about a half cup of soy sauce, a tablespoon of brown sugar, some grated garlic and ginger, and a little ground cinnamon and then heat until the sugar dissolves. Put a couple tablespoons of the mixture in a small bowl and set aside. Dress some chicken thighs in the rest of the sauce and then quickly broil or grill until crisp at the edges and soft within. That happens rather more quickly than you'd think. Serve over the rice, drizzled with the reserved sauce and dusted or sprinkled with a load of chopped scallions and a drift of sesame seeds.

**Tip**

This is fast food essentially; to make it even more so, I most often use boneless, skinless chicken thighs.

**Modifications**

Sometimes I add a little slurry of cornstarch and water, other times a splash of orange juice, occasionally a shot of chili oil to the soy mixture. Turkey cutlets work fairly well in place of the chicken, and the sauce is also quite nice on thick slices of firm tofu.

The New York Times Cooking No-Recipe Recipes

# Buffalo Chicken Dip

I learned about this delicious malarkey from Chris Stanford, a Times colleague who works in London. It's one of those strange, internet-friendly recipes that you could characterize as might-be-disgusting-but-is-actually-good.

Cream cheese

Celery

Hot sauce

Rotisserie chicken

Butter

Blue cheese

Vehicle of choice, such as celery sticks, chips, toast, or tortillas

Melt a bar of cream cheese in a pot and hit it with a big handful of finely diced celery and as much hot sauce as you can manage. Rip apart a rotisserie chicken from the supermarket and fold the shredded meat into the cream cheese sauce, along with maybe some grated Cheddar for tang. Then grease a casserole or pie plate and add the chicken-cheese mixture to it. Dot with crumbled blue cheese and bake at 400°F for 20 to 25 minutes. Serve proudly with celery sticks, chips, toast, or tortillas, and own what you have done. Announce like a president: "This is a recipe from *London*."

# Pressure Cooker Chicken Tacos

There's no one better at the midweek miracle meal than my friend and colleague Melissa Clark, who turned me on to this gem of a recipe. It's best with chicken thighs, ideally the skinless, boneless variety—though skin and bones are fine. So are breasts. So are turkey thighs, for that matter.

Chicken

Tomatoes

Jalapeño

Chile powder

Cumin

Paprika

Tortillas

Cheese

Season a chicken with salt and pepper, then put it in the pressure cooker pot with some chopped tomatoes and a seeded diced jalapeño. Add a tablespoon of chile powder, a little ground cumin, some smoked paprika, and a splash of water. Set the machine to high pressure for 14 minutes, manual release, and then shred the meat back into the sauce and serve with warm tortillas, grated cheese, and whatever else you like.

**Modification**

For a green version, you can add a cup or so of salsa verde to the cooking pot, if you have any around.

# Molasses Fried Chicken

Frying chicken doesn't require a recipe so much as a commitment to best practices: A long bath for the chicken. Flour for the dredge. Hot oil in a pan with high sides. And a rack on which to rest the chicken, because you really ought to cook it twice—once to set the crust and the second time to get it well and truly crunchy, with the meat cooked through.

Chicken

Buttermilk

Molasses

Flour

Chile powder

Red pepper flakes

Paprika

Neutral oil

Once you've got your fried chicken steps sorted, you can start to embellish, as my friend Tahyra does: Soak your chicken parts in buttermilk and add a bloop of molasses to the marinade for the last 30 minutes or so of soaking, which does a great deal more than you may think to promote both sweetness and a golden crust. Then dial up the flour used to coat the chicken by adding both chile powder and red pepper flakes, along with a shake of paprika. It's a fantastic combination. Pour a generous amount of oil into a cast-iron skillet, a couple of inches deep, and set over medium-high heat. Drop a pinch of flour into the skillet and when it sizzles, the oil is ready to go. Fry the chicken twice.

**Tip**

When you're done frying, fish out a quarter cup or so of the cooking fat and combine it with a quarter cup of the leftover flour mixture in a pan. Cook that down into a roux, then hit it with a glug of milk to make a hot flavorful gravy you can serve alongside the chicken.

# Skillet Chicken with Vegetables and Wine

Braised chicken thighs! Serve with couscous, maybe? It's good.

Chicken thighs

Flour

Butter

Neutral oil

Onion

Carrot

Celery

Wine

Thyme

Dust one or two bone-in thighs per person in salt, pepper, and flour, then brown them in an oven-safe skillet in butter and oil. Set them aside and sauté some diced onion, carrot, and celery in the remaining fat, then deglaze the pan with a cup of wine—I use red generally, but white would be great as well. Return the chicken to the pan with some chopped thyme and slide the thing into a 400°F oven to braise and bubble for 30 minutes or so, until the chicken is tender and the skin is crisp. Transfer the chicken to a warm serving platter and reduce the braising liquid on the stove top until it has thickened into a kind of gravy. Spoon over the chicken and tuck in.

# Pan-Roasted Chicken with Chiles

Here is a take on a recipe from the Los Angeles chef Suzanne Goin, whose book *Sunday Suppers at Lucques* is an exacting and delicious guide to restaurant cooking at home. Serve alongside or on top of a pile of baby greens lightly dressed in lemon juice and olive oil, with some bread to mop up the juices.

Chicken thighs

Olive oil

Butter

Thyme

Dried chiles

Fresh bread crumbs (see page 48)

Mustard

Simply brown some skin-on chicken thighs in olive oil and butter over medium heat in an oven-safe skillet, adding lots of fresh thyme leaves and a couple crumbled chiles (I like chiles de árbol). Toss some bread crumbs with melted butter. Apply a thin smear of mustard to each thigh, shower with the bread crumbs, and transfer the pan to the broiler to crisp the chicken into succulence.

# Roasted Chicken Parm

Red-sauce Italian American cooking at its easiest. Sautéed greens go nicely, with plain spaghetti, on the side.

Chicken thighs

Lemon

Red pepper flakes

Olive oil

Canned whole tomatoes

Mozzarella

Parmesan

Basil

Take your chicken thighs, bone-in or boneless—it's your call, but ideally with skin—and put them in a bowl. Shower them with salt, pepper, grated lemon zest, red pepper flakes, and a few glugs of olive oil, then get them on an oiled sheet pan in a 425°F oven, skin-side up, spreading them out as much as you can manage. While the chicken roasts, warm the tomatoes on the stove with a splash of olive oil and a little pepper, crushing them with the back of a spoon. Watch the chicken get truly crisped—it'll take 35 to 40 minutes—and then place a nice slice of mozzarella on each one to melt while still in the oven. (Activate the broiler, if you like, but I prefer the gentle melt.) Spoon warm tomato sauce onto each plate, then top with a cheese-covered chicken thigh, some grated Parmesan, and a few torn basil leaves.

# Chicken with Caramelized Onions and Croutons

My pal, the great New York Times food reporter Julia Moskin, gave me this recipe one day in an instant message when I confessed I had no idea what to make for dinner that night. Now I make this all the time.

Onion

Shallots

Neutral oil

Chicken thighs

Wine or chicken stock

Good bread

Olive oil

Bitter salad greens

Scatter a bunch of sliced onion and shallots across the oiled bottom of a large pan, then put a bunch of bone-in chicken thighs on top of them, skin-side up. Season the thighs with salt and pepper, then slide the pan into a 425°F oven to roast until the chicken is crisp on top and cooked through, about 35 minutes. Shake the pan every so often, and add wine or stock if the onion is browning too fast. Meanwhile, make some croutons from good, chewy olive oil–tossed bread cubes, toasting them in a pan until golden or in the oven on a sheet pan alongside the chicken. They can be cut or torn up—no matter. When everything's done, put the salad greens on a warm platter, top with the croutons, dump the contents of the roasting pan over the top, and arrange the chicken on top of that. Boy howdy.

# Quick-Roasted Chicken with Tarragon

French elegance on the fly. While the chicken is roasting, make some rice or boil off a few potatoes. You can also make a salad or sauté some greens.

Mayonnaise

Dijon mustard

Tarragon

Chicken thighs

Neutral oil

Fresh bread crumbs
(see page 48)

Mix a few tablespoons of mayo with a little Dijon mustard and a lot of chopped tarragon in a large bowl until everything's incorporated to your liking. Salt and pepper some chicken thighs—I'd use bone-in, but boneless would also work—then add the thighs to the mustard mixture, tossing to coat the meat. Arrange the chicken on a greased sheet pan and cover each piece with a handful of bread crumbs, really pressing the crumbs in so they adhere. Slide the pan into a 425°F oven for 30 minutes. Check to see if the chicken is cooked all the way through. Probably not. Another 5 to 10 minutes ought to do it. You're looking for a nice crisp crust, golden brown, around the luscious meat.

# Spiced Duck Breasts with Roasted Eggplant and Rice

I learned this meal—fancy and improvisatory—from the wily kitchen magician Manny Howard, who never uses a recipe.

Rice

Eggplant

Honey

Olive oil

Apple cider vinegar

Garlic

Duck breasts

Five-spice powder

Neutral oil

Scallions

Set a pot of rice cooking. Split small eggplant lengthwise, then crosshatch their interiors without splitting the skin, and paint them with honey cut with a little olive oil and apple cider vinegar. Sprinkle with a bunch of salt and pepper and a few cloves of coarsely chopped garlic. Roast in a hot oven until they start to collapse. While the eggplant's cooking, crosshatch the skin of the breasts as you did the eggplant, cutting deep into the fat. Season the breasts aggressively with salt, pepper, and five-spice powder. Slide the breasts skin-side down into an oil-slicked sauté pan set over medium heat, and slowly toast the spices, allowing the skin to get crisp on what marine engineers call a slow bell. Then turn the breasts over and allow the meat to cook until it is just past rare at the center. Serve thickly sliced with a portion of eggplant, a scoop of rice, and a scattering of sliced scallions across the top.

**Tip**

This recipe may be why ceramic nonstick pans were invented. They're not actually ceramic, of course. They're metal, with a sand-and-silicone coating that is bananas slippery while offering a beautiful sear.

**Modifications**

The steps for the duck preparation work pretty well with chicken thighs, and at a considerably lower price point.

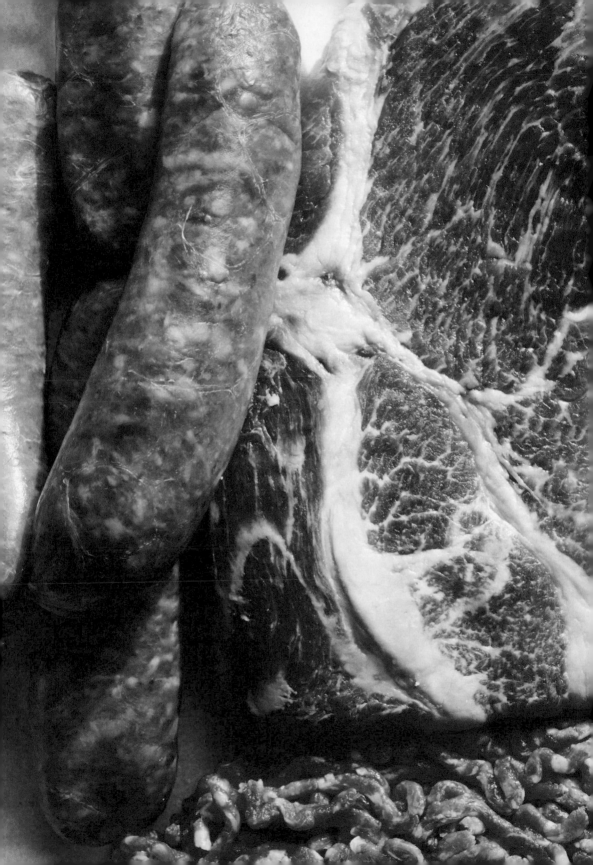

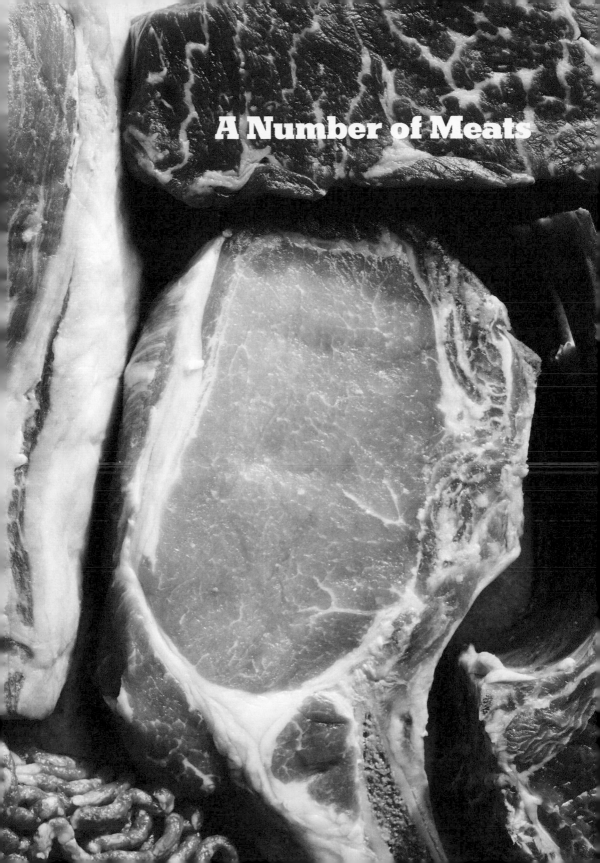

A Number of Meats

# Seared Lamb Chops with Lemon and Butter-Braised Potatoes

Lamb chops are expensive, but they are also delicious and easy to cook. This recipe that is not a recipe is worth the splurge.

Yellow potatoes

Onion

Butter

Chicken stock

Lamb chops

Garlic

Olive oil

Rosemary

Lemons

Cut some yellow potatoes into chunks and put them in a deep skillet set over medium-high heat along with some chopped onion and a few tablespoons of butter. Season with salt and pepper. Cook for about 10 minutes, stirring often, then add enough chicken stock so that the potatoes are almost covered. Bring to a boil, then simmer for 30 minutes until the potatoes are tender. Meanwhile, massage as many lamb chops as you need with minced garlic, salt, pepper, and a little oil. Sear them in a hot cast-iron pan, and finish them in a 425°F oven with rosemary stems or a dusting of dried rosemary and some thinly sliced lemons, until the lamb is just pink inside, about 10 minutes, maybe fewer. Garnish with more rosemary. Serve with potatoes alongside.

**Modification**

If you don't have chicken stock, switch to wine or water.

# Smothered Pork Chops

This is a bulwark against bad weather, one of the great rainy-day feasts. I like it with rice and sautéed greens. And I'm sorry, but if you don't have a Dutch oven, one of those big, heavy numbers in which you can burble beans, bake bread, and make gumbo and stew, I really think you ought to get one. This recipe practically depends on it. You'll have it the rest of your life.

Flour

Your favorite spices

Pork chops

Neutral oil

Butter

Onion

Chicken stock

Bay leaf

Mix some flour with spices—chile powder, salt, pepper, smoked paprika, red pepper flakes, or with Lawry's seasoned salt or Old Bay seasoning. Dredge your chops in this mixture and sear them off in an oil-slicked Dutch oven, reserving the remaining dredging flour, until they're crisp at the edges and brown. Set the chops on a plate. Dump the oil and wipe out the pot. Add some butter and sauté an enormous amount of sliced onions. When the onions wilt and go soft, add a few tablespoons of the leftover dredging flour and cook, stirring often, for 5 minutes or so. Add chicken stock, about a half inch deep, and a bay leaf and stir, then add the pork chops, which will sink into the onion and sauce. Cover the pot and put it in a 350°F oven for 45 minutes to an hour.

**Tips**

Attend to that browning process at the beginning carefully. You want a big flavorful crust on the meat before you braise it, to enhance the taste of the sauce and offer a little texture at the end as well.

The New York Times Cooking No-Recipe Recipes

# Quick-Broiled Pork Chops with Peanuts and Gochujang

Secure the thinnest chops you can find at the store—that's crucial for the quick-broil step. Go with rice on the side.

Peanuts

Sesame oil

Chile powder

Neutral oil

Pork chops

Gochujang

Orange juice

Mirin

Scallions

Throw a few handfuls of dry-roasted peanuts in a pan set over medium-high heat with a glug of sesame oil. Let those go until they're fragrant and just beginning to darken, then take them off the heat and toss with a few shakes of chile powder. Set the peanuts aside and heat your broiler. Line a sheet pan with foil and oil it lightly. Salt and pepper your chops, lay them out on the sheet pan, and slide them into the oven. Broil the chops for about 4 minutes, then flip them over to finish. Meanwhile, mix a tablespoon or so of gochujang with a healthy splash of orange juice and a wisp of mirin. Taste. Adjust. Pour into a deep serving dish or platter. When the chops are well crusted and brown, slide them into the sauce and give a toss. Top with the peanuts and some chopped scallions.

# Hasselback Kielbasa

Serve with steamed greens or a fresh baguette.

Onion

Bell pepper

Neutral oil

Kielbasa

Apricot preserves

Mustard

Get a sheet pan ripping hot in a 425°F oven while you cut up a couple of small onions and a bell pepper or two, whatever color you prefer. Toss the vegetables in a splash of oil, salt and pepper them, and tip them into a single layer on the hot pan. Roast in the oven while you cut the kielbasa into thin slices, stopping short of cutting all the way through the sausage. You want to end up with a long accordion, basically, or an attenuated pill bug. Now remove the vegetables from the oven, give them a stir, and put the kielbasa on top. Return the sheet pan to the oven and roast everything into crisp softness, 20 to 25 minutes, basting heavily two or three times with a mixture of equal parts apricot preserves and mustard, about 2 tablespoons of each.

# Chorizo Nachos

I interviewed the television chef and personality Rachael Ray once, in her studio kitchen at the end of a long day of filming. She poured us glasses of wine and while she was talking, assembled a platter of nachos. I don't remember a thing I asked or a thing she told me, but the nachos have stayed with me. I still make them her way.

Fresh chorizo

Cheddar

American cheese

Cream

Cornstarch

Tortilla chips

Pickled jalapeños

Cilantro

Lime

Crumble fresh chorizo into a hot pan and cook it til it's good and grainy and dark. In a saucepan, melt a fistful of grated Cheddar, a few slices of American cheese, a splash of cream, and a sprinkle of cornstarch. Spread some tortilla chips on a sheet pan and heat in a hot oven for about 10 minutes, which concentrates their flavor beautifully. Distribute the chorizo over the chips. Lash everything with the cheese sauce. Top with slices of pickled jalapeños, showers of chopped cilantro, and wedges of lime.

# Smashed Potatoes with Bacon, Cheddar, and Greens

It's a quintessential no-recipe recipe. There are no rules.

Potatoes

Olive oil

Bacon

Cheddar

Greens

Avocado

Sour cream or yogurt

Get some nice baseball-size, yellow-fleshed potatoes, one per person. Toss them with olive oil, salt, and pepper on a sheet pan and slide them into a hot oven to roast at, say, 425°F. While they're cooking, make yourself useful. Fry some bacon; grate some Cheddar; toss a few large handfuls of spinach or baby kale with olive oil, just enough to lightly coat the leaves; slice some avocados; and take some sour cream or yogurt from the refrigerator. When the potatoes are soft, pull them from the oven and smash them with the bottom of a coffee cup or drinking glass. Arrange the smashed potatoes on the sheet pan in portions. Top each portion with greens, chopped bacon, and plenty of cheese. Return to the oven to melt the cheese. Garnish with avocado and dots of sour cream or yogurt.

### Modifications

You can replace the bacon with merguez. You can use breakfast sausage. Or no meat at all.

# Meatball Salad

This is a salad that I learned how to make at the elbow of the pizza rector Mark Iacono, in the basement of Lucali, his candle-lit restaurant in Carroll Gardens, Brooklyn. Picture meatballs on a pile of torn iceberg lettuce studded with red onion, tomato, black olives, and celery, the whole thing absolutely drenched in a sharp, salty, vinegary dressing pink with tomato juices, like the stuff at the bottom of the salad bowl at the end of a big family dinner. It is crazily delicious.

Ground beef

Milk

Bread crumbs

Butter

Tomato Sauce

Olive oil

Red wine vinegar

Tomatoes

Olives

Red onion

Crunchy lettuce

Celery

Crusty bread

I won't tell you how to make meatballs. You no doubt have your own ideas about that: ground beef and milk-moistened bread crumbs, maybe fried crisp and simmered in buttery tomato sauce. The important thing here is the dressing: olive oil with enough red wine vinegar in it that you're a little nervous about it. Then a lot of salt. Take a small tomato and squeeze it into the bowl. Maybe add a splash of olive brine. Definitely some slivered red onion. Whisk it into an emulsified funk and adjust all dials to 11. It should taste like a cartoon salad dressing, its features larger than life. That goes over cold, chopped iceberg lettuce, some sliced celery tops, quartered tomatoes, olives, and the rest of the slivered onion. Plop your meatballs on top and serve with a hunk of bread. It doesn't sound like much, perhaps. But it's really, really good.

# Curry Goat with Mango Chutney

I grew up eating the food of the West Indian diaspora in Brooklyn, where curry goat is served on the bone. I made a version with ground goat once and it cooked so quickly and beautifully that I did so again and again—a weeknight hack that's paid dividends for years. Serve the dish with rice cooked with coconut milk in place of water.

Bacon

Ground goat meat

Onion

Garlic

Ginger

Jalapeño

Curry powder

Allspice

Chicken stock

Mango chutney

Hot sauce

Fry a little bacon in your pan to give the dish a fatty bass note, then add some ground goat meat, and then the diced onion, and minced garlic, ginger, and jalapeño. Hit the sizzling mixture with a bunch of curry powder and some crushed allspice berries (or a pinch of ground), and a healthy splash of chicken stock. Let it simmer as if you were making sloppy joes. Add a few tablespoons of mango chutney at the end, and a few shakes of hot sauce to offset the sweet.

**Modification**

You can use ground lamb instead of goat, or beef or pork. Undoubtedly, you could also use crumbled tofu or seitan instead.

# Cafeteria Tacos

Remember those tacos served at your school's cafeteria in their crisp, golden shells? Maybe you liked them. I loved them. I can make you love them, too.

Onion

Garlic

Jalapeño

Neutral oil

Ground beef

Chile powder

Cumin

Cornstarch

Canned tomatoes

Chicken stock

Tortillas

Toppings, such as shredded lettuce, cheese, sour cream, and salsa

Fry a diced onion, some garlic, and a diced jalapeño in oil in a large pan set over medium-high heat, then add some 20-percent fat ground beef and break it up in the pan. Cook until it has started to crisp around the edges, then add a couple of tablespoons of chile powder, a healthy shake of ground cumin, some salt and pepper, and a tablespoon of cornstarch. (Yes, cornstarch.) Let that cook for a minute, then tip a can of diced tomatoes into the pan. Stir to combine, let it cook down for a few minutes, and then add some chicken stock (or water, if you don't have any stock) and watch as the gravy around the meat thickens. Cook for 10 to 15 minutes on low and then use it as the filling for your tortillas, hard-shell or not, topped with lettuce, cheese, sour cream, and salsa, or whatever else you like.

# Cowboy Ragu

In South Texas and northern Mexico, cowboys make this dish on a disco—
a harrow blade with its center welded shut and ground smooth, mounted
on legs and set over a fire like a wok. You can use a large sauté pan and your
regular stove in its place. It's serial cooking and a good dish to eat outside,
if you can, standing around with friends and scooping from the pan into
warm buns or tortillas.

Ground beef

Fresh chorizo

Onion

Green bell pepper

Garlic

Canned tomatoes

Chipotle chiles
in adobo

Beer

Hot dog buns

Cheese

First, sauté some ground beef and chorizo in a big
pan. Add a few fistfuls of chopped onion and green
bell pepper and a couple of cloves of minced garlic.
Then add a can of diced tomatoes and their juice, a
couple of chipotle chiles, and some of their adobo
sauce. Then add a beer to loosen things up and some
salt to sharpen all the flavors. Spoon into buns, add
a cloak of grated cheese, and serve.

**Modifications**

Pork for the beef works
nicely, and so does crumbled
tofu. I like the chipotles for
their smokiness, but plain
chopped jalapeños work
as well. And the beer's just
a rhetorical flourish. You
can use stock or water in
its place.

# Meat Sauce and Eggs

Read twice, then cook.

Ground beef and/or sausage

Olive oil

Onion and/or hot pepper

Garlic

Canned tomatoes

Tortilla or corn chips

Eggs

Cheese

Take a handful of ground beef if you have that, or crumble up some sausage, or use both. Whatever the protein, heat it through in hot olive oil and follow it up with some diced onion, or diced hot pepper, or both, and a garlic clove or two. Get this mixture of invention soft and crisp at once and then tip a can of whole tomatoes into the mixture and break them up with the back of a spoon. Let that simmer awhile and then add a handful of tortilla or corn chips, or not. Now season with salt and then create a few little divots in the sauce. Crack an egg into each of these. Sprinkle some shredded cheese over the top and cover the pan for 3 to 4 minutes, until the egg whites have just set but the yolks are still runny and soft, a perfect velvet to stir into the whole. That's a fine affair.

### Modifications

Instead of the ground beef and the sausage, you can dice some bacon. Or you can shred a little cooked chicken. Have some leftover cooked white rice but no chips? Serving over rice could work, too. If you don't have any of those things, prepare some toast to go along with the finished dish. It's your recipe.

# New Mexican Hot Dish

I've been cooking enchiladas con carne ever since Robb Walsh taught me how to make them in the kitchen of his El Real Tex-Mex Cafe in Houston. But I can't say I make them the way he taught me any longer. Enchiladas can be a drag to assemble. So I do as New Mexicans do, and stack rather than roll.

Ground beef

Neutral oil

Flour

Onions

Garlic

Jalapeño

Chile powder

Cumin

Oregano

Tomatoes

Corn tortillas

Sour cream

Cheese

Salsa

Sauté a pound or so of ground beef in a splash of oil, with a little flour and a pinch of salt, and then spoon out the beef and set it aside. Use the same pan, adding a glug of oil, to cook some chopped onion, garlic, and jalapeño. Return the meat to the pan and hit it with chile powder, ground cumin, and oregano. Add chopped fresh tomatoes and a little water to loosen everything up, then let it reduce a little. That's my chili. Meanwhile, get the oven hot and grab a casserole dish, some corn tortillas and a mixture of grated cheese—I go mostly Cheddar and a little American. Sue me. Put a little chili in the bottom of the casserole, warm the tortillas in a dry skillet, and lay them across the chili as if building the first layer of a lasagna. Then do that again and again, and finish with the remaining chili and the cheese. Bake at 350°F in the oven until everything's bubbling. Serve with chopped raw onions, sour cream, and salsa on the side. Enchilada casserole, hon. I'm telling you, you could make it tonight.

# Meatloaf

Making meatloaf without a recipe is good fun and self-affirming to boot. For an improvisatory recipe, this one reads especially bossy, even for me. I'll give you the executive summary: You want the loaf to be moist with fats, so that the finished dish is not dry but packed with flavor. This makes for a fantastic dinner alongside mashed potatoes and sweet peas.

Ground meat

Shallots

Egg

Bread crumbs
(see page 48)

Milk

Bacon

Neutral oil

Ketchup

Hot sauce

Gather ground beef and ground pork, about a half pound of each, along with a couple of shallots (or small onions!), an egg from a pampered chicken, some bread crumbs from the back of the cupboard, a splash of milk to moisten them, and plenty of salt and pepper. I get kind of fancy about it. I dice the shallots fine so that they almost dissolve into the meat. Add some diced bacon for fat and flavor, or a little high-fat butter or nothing at all. Combine all that. Shape into a loaf and put it on a lightly oiled sheet pan. Do I deploy my squeeze bottle of ketchup cut with Texas Pete hot sauce to anoint the top of the loaf in the way fancy sushi chefs do their dragon rolls? I do. Bake at 375°F for a little more than 30 minutes. You'll sleep like a kitten after dinner.

**Tip**

The loaf should be neither too flat nor too towering, but instead a pleasant form that reminds you of a loaf of good homemade bread. I don't recommend using a loaf pan. This recipe has a lot of fat in it. You want some to run off.

**Modification**

You can use ground turkey, veal, venison, lamb, or sausage instead of beef and pork. If I have pork rillettes and country pâté in the fridge, I put a little of those into the mix as well.

# Sloppy Joes

I like steamed broccoli on the side, a walk for the dog, and bed.

Olive oil

Onion

Celery

Jalapeño

Red bell pepper

Garlic

Ground beef

Tomato paste

Canned tomato sauce

Worcestershire sauce

Hot sauce

Hamburger buns

Put a Dutch oven over medium-high heat on your stove, then add a glug of olive oil and sauté a handful of chopped onion, a couple diced ribs of celery, a diced jalapeño, and a diced small red bell pepper. When the mixture is super-soft, add a few cloves of minced garlic and cook for a couple more minutes. Dump a pound and a half of ground beef into the pot—ideally the sort that is 20 percent fat—and stir and sizzle until it is well browned, about 10 minutes. Bring the heat down a bit and add a lot of tomato paste—say a few tablespoons, maybe a quarter cup—and let it get a little toasty before adding a cup or more of canned tomato sauce. Cook that down for a few minutes, then add quite a few glugs of Worcestershire sauce and hot sauce and continue cooking until the mixture is quite thick, another 15 or 20 minutes. Season with salt. Toast some buns, load them up, and set in.

A Number of Meats

# Curry Beef

This is curry beef as cooked in dorm rooms and the galleys of fishing boats far out to sea. A fantastic easy meal when all you want is flavor, fast.

Rice

Garlic

Ginger

Onion

Neutral oil

Beef stew meat

Curry powder

Potato

Carrot

Chicken stock

Mango chutney

Start a pot of rice. Chop a bunch of garlic and ginger and an onion into the finest sort of dice, then sauté it all golden in oil. Add some cubed beef and allow it to sizzle and brown. Shake in some of your favorite curry powder. Let it get going good, then add cubes of potato and carrot, enough chicken stock to cover, and a spoonful or two of mango chutney. Allow it to cook down into gravy, then serve it all over a scoop of rice. This is easy work with a powerful payoff.

**Tip**

This is a recipe that relies on a spice mix—generally built on a foundation of cumin, coriander, and turmeric—that is made differently all over the world. I most often use a West Indian variety, heavy on the turmeric. It's commonly labeled "Jamaican curry powder."

The New York Times Cooking No-Recipe Recipes

# Celery and Beef Stir-Fry with Gochujang

Celery and beef love each other very much, especially in this fast and loose stir-fry that recalls but does not replicate a classic Sichuan dish with a fantastic name—Send the Rice Down. I serve it with noodles.

Chinese egg noodles

Celery

Ground beef

Neutral oil

Gochujang or spicy chili-bean paste

Ginger

Soy sauce

Black vinegar

Cook the noodles as directed on the package, then drain and set aside. Dice a couple stalks of celery, then quickly blanch them in simmering water and drain, running them under cold water to stop their cooking. Shake dry and set aside. Then cook a little bit of ground beef in a wok slicked with oil and, when it's no longer pink and watery but starting to crisp and bubble, hit it with a big, sloppy tablespoon or two of gochujang. Cook that for a while, stir-frying, then add a few tablespoons of minced ginger to the mix. Stir and fry, then add the blanched celery, let it get hot. Serve over the noodles, drizzled with a little soy sauce and a spray of black vinegar.

**Tip**

If you cook the celery in the morning, before attending to your daily affairs, dinner in the evening will go that much faster. The blanched celery keeps well in the fridge for the day.

**Modifications**

Ground lamb or pork works as well as the beef. So does crumbled firm tofu, though going with it may call for using a little more oil. No gochujang? Use chili-bean paste.

# Steak Tacos with Pineapple Salsa

There are times when there's a sale on skirt steak, and it's almost as cheap as it used to be before everyone started cooking it and its price rose to the top of the sky. This is the recipe for when that happens.

Skirt steak

Pineapple

Pickled jalapeños

Chile powder

Cilantro

Tortillas

Cheese

Take your skirt steak out of the refrigerator. Make salsa from fresh or canned pineapple, pickled jalapeños, and a healthy couple shakes of chile powder, along with plenty of chopped cilantro. Shower the meat with salt and pepper and broil it for 2 to 3 minutes a side until perfect and rare. Warm some corn tortillas. Grate some Cheddar. Rest the steak for 5 minutes or so. Slice it, and serve with the tortillas, cheese, and that awesome salsa. Anyone want to watch a movie after dinner? For once, there's time for that.

# Dessert, Please

# Oven S'mores

You don't need a campfire.

Graham crackers

Marshmallows

Chocolate bars

Arrange a few lines of graham crackers on a sheet pan and top half with marshmallows and squares of chocolate. Bake at 400°F until the marshmallows are puffed and golden and the chocolate is a little melty. Top each with another graham cracker, squeeze the sandwich lightly, and serve.

**Modification**

Spread raspberry jam on the top graham crackers and place them on the sandwiches jam-side down.

# Bananas Foster

Bananas sautéed in butter, then flamed with rum? What could possibly go wrong? Serve with vanilla ice cream.

Unsalted butter

Brown sugar

Bananas

Dark rum

Melt a lot of unsalted butter in a sauté pan with a big sprinkling of brown sugar. When the mixture foams, add some peeled and halved bananas and sauté them until lightly browned. Add a jigger of dark rum to the pan and tilt it away from you. The stove's flame will ignite the alcohol in a righteous woosh. Carefully spoon the sauce over the bananas until the flames go out.

**Tip**

If you don't have a gas stove, use a lighter wand to ignite the rum in the pan.

# Vegan Banana Ice Cream

I like bananas after dinner. Everyone likes ice cream. Win-win.

Bananas

Peanuts

Slice some bananas in the morning and put them in a resealable bag in the freezer. Come evening, put those banana slices into a food processor and whiz them up into an ice cream that has no cream. Scoop and top with some chopped peanuts. That's it!

**Modifications**

Add a splash of maple syrup to the whizzed-up bananas, if you like. You can top with pecans instead of peanuts. Or chopped fruit. Or both. Finish with a squirt of real whipped cream?

# Watermelon Granita

Is it possible to improve on the deliciousness of a slice of cold watermelon? Yes, it is.

Watermelon

Sugar

Lime

There are a number of ways to make this granita, but my favorite is to cut watermelon into chunks, discard the rind, and put the pieces in a bag in the freezer for a few hours. Then blitz them in a blender or food processor and hit them with a little sugar and lime juice. That yields a super-slushy situation that's looser than your traditional granita. If you'd like to firm it up, pour the mixture into a shallow dish and put it in the freezer for an hour or so longer.

**Modification**

Don't freeze the watermelon in advance; do that after you've blitzed it with the sugar and lime juice. Pour the mixture into a shallow dish and put it in the freezer for two or three hours. Rake with a fork every hour or so. Then spoon out the rakings into bowls and serve.

# Strawberry Sundaes with Hot Fudge

Here's light work that results in unfettered joy for many. The fudge beats the jarred stuff from the bodega or supermarket by a considerable margin. And you can store what you don't eat in the refrigerator, in a covered jar, for tomorrow night. To rewarm, give a spoonful or two a few seconds in the microwave and you're back in action.

Cocoa powder

Sugar

Cream

Unsalted butter

Vanilla extract

Strawberry ice cream

The fudge is easy as long as you keep the ratios right: a cup each of cocoa powder, white sugar, and cream, whisked together over medium heat; a stick of unsalted butter, stirred in by pats until everything's velvety; a glug of vanilla and you're good to go. Drizzle that over a couple scoops of ice cream, maybe with some actual strawbos as garnish, and call the evening a win.

# Acknowledgments

This book owes its existence to NYT Cooking and to all those at The New York Times who work to make it shine, on stage and off. I owe particular gratitude to my principal editors, Krysten Chambrot and Mark Josephson, who have been with the no-recipe recipe project from the start, as well as to the photo editor Kim Gougenheim, who first introduced me to the powerful work of the photographer David Malosh and the genius food styling of Simon Andrews. Those two men are magicians.

Without Emily Weinstein and Amanda Rottier, our stalwart and clear-eyed leaders, the book would never have progressed beyond a notion. Without Cynthia Cannell and Caroline Que, it would never have become a proposal. And without Lorena Jones and the fine crew at Ten Speed Press along with The Times design chieftan Kelly Doe, it would never have become an actual living thing. I thank them all, unreservedly, acknowledging that if there are errors in here, they're mine. I hope you enjoy dinner.

# About the Author

Sam Sifton is an assistant managing editor of The New York Times, responsible for culture and lifestyle coverage, and the founding editor of NYT Cooking. Formerly the national news editor, restaurant critic, and culture editor, he joined The Times in 2002 after stints at *Talk* magazine, *New York Press*, and *American Heritage* magazine. He is the author of *Thanksgiving: How to Cook It Well* and *See You on Sunday: A Cookbook for Family and Friends.*

# Index